Co Armagh & Co Antrim

Edited by Aimée Vanstone

 Young**Writers**

First published in Great Britain in 2008 by:
Young Writers
Remus House
Coltsfoot Drive
Peterborough
PE2 9JX
Telephone: 01733 890066
Website: www.youngwriters.co.uk

SB ISBN 978-1 84431 479 9

Foreword

Young Writers was established in 1991 and has been passionately devoted to the promotion of reading and writing in children and young adults ever since. The quest continues today. Young Writers remains as committed to the nurturing of poetic and literary talent as ever.

This year's Young Writers competition has proven as vibrant and dynamic as ever and we are delighted to present a showcase of the best poetry from across the UK and in some cases overseas. Each poem has been selected from a wealth of *Little Laureates* entries before ultimately being published in this, our sixteenth primary school poetry series.

Once again, we have been supremely impressed by the overall quality of the entries we have received. The imagination, energy and creativity which has gone into each young writer's entry made choosing the poems a challenging and often difficult but ultimately hugely rewarding task - the general high standard of the work submitted ensured this opportunity to bring their poetry to a larger appreciative audience.

We sincerely hope you are pleased with this final collection and that you will enjoy *Little Laureates Co Armagh & Co Antrim* for many years to come.

Contents

Louise Compston (11)   17
Gavin Meehan (9)   18
Hannah Murphy (10)   18
Rachel Connolly (9)   19
Conor Hanna (9)   19
Siva O'Neill (11)   20
Rebecca Connolly (7)   20
Jayne Nelson (10)   21
Nicole Weir (11)   21
Rhiannon Quinn-Nixon (10)   22
Aaron Pollock (8)   22
James Goldsmith (10)   23
Emma Ross (10)   23
Thomas Earley (7)   24
Alysia Rea (7)   24
William Burke (7)   24
Tom Polly (10)   25
Layna Morelli (7)   25
Dillon Edgar-Lee (8)   25
Aoife Polly (10)   26
Matthew Sullivan (8)   26
Zak Earley (7)   26
Stefan Angelone (10)   27
Martin Kelley (10)   27
Marie Toner (9)   27
Chloe Hanna (10)   28
Jack Creaner (10)   28
Gerard Loughran (9)   28
Chloe Campbell (10)   29
Ande Peden (10)   29

Currie Primary School, Belfast
Hayley Dodds (8)   30
Paul Robinson (7)   30
Dylan Johnston (7)   30
Leon Glass (7)   31
Britney Mason (7)   31
Cameron Ferris (7)   31
Brennan Sime (8)   32

Garryduff Primary School, Ballymoney

Adam Clyde (10)	
Andrew Young (11)	32
Lucy Hassan (9)	32
Nicole Milliken (10)	32
Lucy Buick (10)	33
Rebecca Macabe (10)	33
Peter Beattie (11)	33
Adam Patrick (8)	33
Emma Hutchison (10)	34
Andrew Hutchinson (9)	34
Stephanie Love (8)	34
Jenny Love (10)	35
Jack McMullan (9)	35
Elizabeth Gaston (8)	35
Charlotte Calderwood (10)	36
Lucy Gaston (10)	36
Justine McNougher (11)	36
	36

Kingsmills Primary School, Armagh

Alison Gamble (10)	
Ryan Walker (10)	37
Deborah King (10)	37
Danielle Hazley (8)	37
Robert Ferris (8)	38
Alistair Marks (10)	38
David Cartmill (10)	38
Amy Cartmill (10)	39
Killian Walker (9)	39
Kyle Rogers (9)	39
Hannah Brady (11)	40
Adam Copeland (10)	40
Lucy Bell (11)	41
Nicole Brady (8)	41
Andrew Hamilton (8)	42
Thomas Ferris (10)	42
	43

Maghaberry Primary School, Craigavon

Lesley Thompson (11)	
Nathan Harper (9)	43
Catherine Courtney (10)	43
	44

Our Lady's & St Mochua's Primary School, Derrynoose

Emma-Kate Haughey (9)   58
Carolyn Fitzpatrick (9)   58
Alice Lennon (9)   59
Catherine Nugent (9)   60
Gabrielle Fox (9)   60
Michael McGrane (11)   61
Olivia McKearney (10)   61
Shannon McGuigan (10)   62
Keelin Boyd (10)   62
Ellen Hamilton (9)   63
Hannah Finnegan (10)   63
Marie-Claire Burke (10)   64
Ryan Murray (11)   64
Eryn Murphy (9)   64
Peter Parker (10)   65
Kevin McKenna (10)   65
Sinead McKee (10)   65
Ciara Woods (10)   66
Amanda Tomany (11)   66

Portadown Integrated Primary School, Portadown
Juliette Roberts (7)   66
Abigail Uprichard (8)   67
Caoimhe Cullen (8)   67
Aidan Cairns (10)   68
Hallie Adams (8)   68
Jessica Alexander (10)   69
Cliodhna Morgan (9)   69
Niall Magee (10)   70
Cian Murtagh (9)   71
Julia Camporese (10)   72
Nadine McNally (9)   72
Laura Gill (9)   73
Keelan Leeper (9)   73
Allister McCord (9)   74
Megan McLaughlin (8)   74
Christopher Adams (10)   75
Sasha Thompson (9)   75
Sarah Taylor (9)   76
Rachel Kitchen (10)   76
Abigail Tedford (10)   77

Jack Richards (9)   77
Shannon Campbell (10)   78
Jamie Lunt (10)   79

St Bernadette's Primary School, Belfast

Deborah McCluskey (9)   79
Anna Keenan (8)   80
Aimée Maguire (8)   80
Nicole Muir (8)   80
Annalise Warnock (9)   81
Aisling Thompson (9)   81

St Bride's Primary School, Belfast

Grace Guinness (7)   81
Rohan O'Hare (7)   82
Niall Agnew (7)   82
Peter Heaney (7)   83
Callum Herity (8)   83
Anna Sutherland (8)   84
David Connolly (7)   84
Tom Maguire (7)   84
Damian Magee (8)   85
Abhirami Santhosh Pillai (7)   85
Emer Megarity (7)   85
Ara McCartan (8)   86
Paul Armstrong (8)   86
Chloe Ireland (7)   87
Nikol Staikidou (8)   87

St Malachy's Primary School, Newry

Aoife Hollywood (7)   88
Roisin Cranney (8)   88

St Mary's Primary School, Cushendall

Christopher McLaughlin (8)   89
Conall McAteer (8)   90
Molly McLaughlin (8)   91
Holly Fleet (9)   92
Ciaran Quinn (9)   93
Declan Thompson (9)   94

Cliodhna McManus (8)   95
Siobhan McKillop (8)   96
Orlaith McAlister (10)   97
Paul Emerson (10)   97
Liam Gillan (8)   98
Tegan Walker (9)   99
Oran McCarthy (9)   100
Jane Emerson (9)   101
Roisin Healy (10)   102
Fiona McDonnell (9)   102
Daniel O'Boyle (8)   103
Orla Delargy (9)   104
Scott Walsh (8)   105
Lauren Ghio (8)   106

St Oliver Plunkett's Primary School, Toomebridge
Danaé Marron (10)   106
Jamie Donaghy (9)   107
Niamh Bovill (9)   107
Elena Hill (10)   108
Bryan Letters (9)   109
Clodagh Scullion (9)   110
Paul Tohill (10)   111
James McFall (10)   112
Shannon McCann (10)   113
Luke McCoy (9)   113

St Patrick's Primary School, Aughacommon
Dione Kelly (10)   113
Fearghal Hosty-Blaney (10)   114
Megan Doyle (10)   114
Matthew McCabe (10)   114
Meadhbh O'Neill (10)   115
Caolan Farrell (10)   115
Eimear Neeson (10)   115
Liam Coleman (9)   116
Aoibhin McCarron (10)   116
Callum Doran (10)   116
Kerry McGibbon (9)   117
Wiktoria Wylecial (9)   117
Jane Douglas (9)   117

Saints & Scholars Integrated Primary
& Nursery School, Armagh

Strand Primary School, Belfast

The Poems

Autumn

Taste autumn in the woods
Where the squirrels gather their food.
Taste autumn at our school,
Where the children kick the leaves.

Taste autumn in the sky
When the birds fly away.
Taste autumn in the fields
Where the farmer cuts his crops.

Lewis Verner (9)
Ballytober Primary School, Bushmills

Autumn Taste

Taste autumn in the forest
As the squirrels run about with nuts.
Taste autumn in the sky,
As swallows sing a lullaby.

Taste autumn in the fields
As the farmers harvest their crops.
Taste autumn in the garden
As the leaves fall.

Megan Scott (8)
Ballytober Primary School, Bushmills

Autumn Time

Taste autumn in the gardens
As the hedgehogs run under the hedge.
Taste autumn in the wood
And see the leaves fall off the trees.

Taste autumn in the fields
As the farmer cuts the crops.
Taste autumn in the sky
As the birds fly away.

Sam Ramage (8)
Ballytober Primary School, Bushmills

Signs Of Autumn

Taste autumn in the trees
As the leaves turn different colours.
Taste autumn in the forests
As the squirrels gather their nuts.

Taste autumn in the garden
As the hedgehogs cover themselves with leaves and hibernate.
Taste autumn in the sky
As the wind blows and the birds migrate.

Callum Jennings (8)
Ballytober Primary School, Bushmills

Autumn

Taste autumn in the forest
Where squirrels gather their acorns.
Taste autumn in the sky
Where the birds migrate.

Taste autumn in the forest
Where all the leaves turn different colours.
Taste autumn in the fields
Where the farmers dig up all their crops.

Shannon McKay (9)
Ballytober Primary School, Bushmills

Autumn

Taste autumn in the sky
As the birds go flying by.
Taste autumn in the garden
As we rake up the different coloured leaves.

Taste autumn in the fields
As the barley gets cut down.
Taste autumn in the air
As it gets much colder.

James McCullough (9)
Ballytober Primary School, Bushmills

Autumn

Taste autumn in the forest
As the squirrels gather their nuts.
Taste autumn in the garden
Where the leaves are brightly coloured.

Taste autumn in the sky
As the sky turns darker.
Taste autumn on the farm
As the crops are harvested.

Isaac Dunn (8)
Ballytober Primary School, Bushmills

In The Autumn

Taste autumn in the sky
As the birds fly away.
Taste autumn in the country
As the leaves fade away.

Taste autumn in the garden
As the frogs hide away.
Taste autumn in the woods
Where the hedgehogs hide away.

Jordan Bradley (9)
Ballytober Primary School, Bushmills

Autumn

Taste autumn in the park
As the leaves fly by.
Taste autumn on the farm
Where the combines cut the corn.

Taste autumn in the garden
As the children play.
Taste autumn in the forest
As the leaves fall down.

Stuart Nelson (8)
Ballytober Primary School, Bushmills

My Magic Box

(Based on 'Magic Box' by Kit Wright)

I will put in my box . . .
A laugh shared with everybody,
The wettest tear running down my cheek,
A warm hand against mine keeping me safe.

I will put in my box . . .
A terrible storm blowing over a landscape,
A fairy story to help you sleep,
A horrifying nightmare during the night.

I will put in my box . . .
A fairy dancing round and round,
A fire burning the universe,
Basking on a sun-kissed beach on a tropical island.

I will put in my box . . .
A tenth planet and a blue girl,
A crocodile singing High School Musical 2,
A dinosaur doing hip hop.

My box is fashioned from crystals, glass and diamonds,
With rubies on the lid and memories inside.
It's the perfect place for all my secrets.

I shall dream in my box
And fly to Heaven to meet the angels,
Then meet the fairy queen herself.
Then I will fall back down to Earth.

Catherine McGarry (8)
Cranmore Integrated Primary School, Belfast

My Pet

My dragon's head is larger than a skyscraper.
His eyes shine brighter than the light.
His skin is bumpy like the stairs.
His breath is hotter than racing car wheels,
But he's my nice pet!

Graham Kerr (8)
Cranmore Integrated Primary School, Belfast

My Magic Box

(Based on 'Magic Box' by Kit Wright)

I will put in my box . . .
A solid gold fish with silver wings,
Cows' heads and pigs' noses.
A witch with a novelty head.

I will put in my box . . .
A snowman with a freezing cold belly,
The coldest water from the coldest river,
A sixth season with freezing trees.

I will put in my box . . .
A cowboy with a tutu
And a ballerina with a cowboy's hat.
An uncle catching fish and a crocodile watching TV

I will put in my box . . .
The taste of chocolate as it melts down your chinny, chin, chin,
The sound of firewood burning,
The sound of drums banging.

My box is made from solid gold,
Corners are secrets and
Only I know there is a ruby on top.

I shall use my box to take me
To a Manchester United match
And Manchester will win 5-3,
And I will travel back delighted.

Joel Spence (9)
Cranmore Integrated Primary School, Belfast

My Pet

My dragon's head is taller than a volcano.
His eyes glow darker than thunder.
His scales are tougher than rocks.
His breath is hotter than a roaring tornado,
But he's my favourite pet!

Jason Baguio (7)
Cranmore Integrated Primary School, Belfast

My Magic Box
(Based on 'Magic Box' by Kit Wright)

I will put in my box . . .
All my weekends when I am off school,
My computer with my Doctor Who game,
All my surprises from my mum and dad when I am good.

I will put in my box . . .
My dog to stay with us,
Good behaviour so I do not get into trouble,
Dinosaurs because I miss then when I am at school.

I will put in my box . . .
Jurassic Park, my DVD,
Fish fingers, my favourite dinner,
The playground where I love to play.

My box is fashioned from gold,
With diamonds on the lid
And magical powers inside.

I shall fly in my box
With wings up high,
And Aaron beside me.

Andrew McCullough (8)
Cranmore Integrated Primary School, Belfast

My Snow Poem

When I went to bed last night
Snow started to fall in the silvery moonlight.
When I woke up the ground was white,
So me and my brother had a snowball fight.

After that we went inside,
We tripped on the mat and fell on our behinds.
When we got up, our bums were sore,
So we jumped on our beds and gave a big *zzzzzzz*.

Katherine Anne O'Neill-Robinson (9)
Cranmore Integrated Primary School, Belfast

My Magic Box

(Based on 'Magic Box' by Kit Wright)

I will put in my box . . .
The card of Frank Lampard,
The brain of a pig,
The feather of a raven.

I will put in my box . . .
The taste of Aero Bubbles,
The straw of a scarecrow with a funny hat,
A really scary big skeleton playing the guitar.

I will put in my box . . .
The rib cage of a body,
The light of the moon,
The scales of a crocodile.

My box is fashioned from wool, wood, bark,
With bubbles in the corners.
It's big, fluffy and cool.

I shall fight with King Arthur in my box,
And I shall win.

Calum McKeown (9)
Cranmore Integrated Primary School, Belfast

Glamorous Things Abound

G is for glamour, pretty as pink
L is for loveliest glitzy blue eyes
A is for angel, beautiful and kind
M is for modelling fancy clothes around town
O is for orchid, colourful and bright
R is for random, picking out make-up from every shelf
O is for original style, chat and walk
U is for uplifting, cheerful and bright
S is for scent, a pleasant smell of vanilla and fruits.

Rebekah Wynn (9)
Cranmore Integrated Primary School, Belfast

My Magic Box

(Based on 'Magic Box' by Kit Wright)

I will put in my box . . .
A cold, frosty snowman sitting on soft snowy ground,
A gentle cat with beautiful fur dripping from its body,
A soft, gentle teddy bear to snuggle in the night with.

I will put in my box . . .
A beautiful dog with long shaggy hair,
A family to keep me nice and safe,
A limo to take me places.

I will put in my box . . .
A mansion with diamond chandeliers,
A cat in a fish bowl and a fish in a cat's bed,
A stock of Horrid Henry and Harry Potter books.

I will put in my box . . .
All the sweets, vegetables and fruit in the world,
A relaxing bed to dream happy memories in,
My best friends to keep me happy.

My box is made from steel, gold and diamonds sprinkled all over,
Memories with love all around it.

I shall swim in my box in the Olympics
Against the best swimmers in the world
And finish in the limo
To take me home to my box.

Megan Graham (8)
Cranmore Integrated Primary School, Belfast

My Pet

My dragon's head is larger than a school.
His eyes shine like the bright blue sky.
His claws are sharp like razor blades.
His breath is disgusting like rats' caves.
His gigantic tail thrashes like thunder,
But he's fun!

Rebecca Jackson (7)
Cranmore Integrated Primary School, Belfast

My Magic Box

(Based on 'Magic Box' by Kit Wright)

I will put in my box . . .
The taste of a big cream cake,
A man hanging on a roof,
A plastic skeleton cooking on Hallowe'en night,
The taste of love,
A happy family's happy memories.

I will put in my box . . .
A cat driving a car,
A man sleeping in a cat's bed,
A dragon's breath breathing on your face,
A cold and frosty snowman,
The brain of a fish,
A red and yellow Earth
And a blue and green sun.

I will put in my box . . .
The smell of nice roses in a park,
A flock of birds
And a flock of sheep.

My box is fashioned from metal, gold, rubber and steel
With ruby rings on the lid.

I shall walk in my box for ever and ever
And explore.

Jack McArdle (8)
Cranmore Integrated Primary School, Belfast

My Pet

My dragon's head is larger than a building.
His eyes are like glowing bricks.
His tail is sharper than razor blades.
His claws are powerful like tornadoes.
His breath is like rotten fish,
But he's my pal.

Darren Sangster (8)
Cranmore Integrated Primary School, Belfast

My Magic Box

(Based on 'Magic Box' by Kit Wright)

I will put in my box . . .
The taste of chocolate melting in the sun,
The smell of chips cooking in the fryer,
The feeling of a feather blowing in the air.

I will put in my box . . .
The feeling of play dough because it is soft and smooth,
The smell of the nicest ice lolly in the world,
The feeling of a conker rolling up your arm.

I will put in my box . . .
A roundabout that has five diamonds around it,
A ball that can bounce 100 feet high,
A snowball that cannot melt.

My box is fashioned from gold, pink and purple,
With a diamond lid.
Its front and back are pink
With stars all around it.

I shall put in lots of amusement rides.
I will ride all the rides
And take all my friends and family.

Hannah Murtagh (8)
Cranmore Integrated Primary School, Belfast

Christmas

C is for Christmas trees in houses everywhere
H is for happy children
R is for Rudolph and his big red nose
I is for icy icicles
S is for Santa and his little helpers
T is for turkey for Christmas dinner
M is for musical carol singers
A is for angels on top of the tree
S is for snow which I play in.

Scott Hartness (10)
Cranmore Integrated Primary School, Belfast

My Magic Box

(Based on 'Magic Box' by Kit Wright)

I will put in my box . . .
The smell of roses in a fresh garden,
The feel of a soft cat lying on a sofa,
The laugh of my mum.

I will put in my box . . .
The sound of the wind and trees blowing against each other,
The sound of a lake swishing in the wind,
The sound of birds flapping fast.

I will put in my box . . .
A dog in a collar
And a cat on a lead,
And a boy who flies on a carrot.

My box is fashioned from silver, gold and steel,
And the box is purple with red hearts all over.
Its lid is purple with hearts.

I shall walk in my box for ever and ever.
I shall put my good money in it.

Rebekah Sloss (9)
Cranmore Integrated Primary School, Belfast

My Spooky Hallowe'en Poem

H   is for holiday which we get at Hallowe'en
A   is for all the candy you get
L   is for the lines in the apples from the pennies
L   is for laughter you get out of trick or treating
O   is for owls that go tu-whit tu-whoo on the great night
W   is for all the girls who dress up as witches
E   is for the enjoyment you get collecting candy
E   is for the evening off you have with your family
N   is for the night which gives us great fun.

Matthew Blain (9)
Cranmore Integrated Primary School, Belfast

My Magic Box

(Based on 'Magic Box' by Kit Wright)

I will put in my box . . .
The tastes of the sweetest strawberry and its juice running
down my chin,

The taste of the sourest orange
And the fire that the hunter makes.

I will put in my box . . .
The feeling of melted chocolate slipping out of my hand,
The feeling of the crunchiest leaf off the smoothest tree,
The emotions of happy memories.

I will put in my box . . .
A baby-blue sky,
A bright yellow sun,
The lovely dark green grass.

My box is fashioned from colours and gold
With love all over and secrets in every corner.

I shall ski up and down the high mountains of Switzerland in my box
And swim the deepest pool.

Chelsea-Leigh Swift (9)
Cranmore Integrated Primary School, Belfast

My Best Friend Is My Mum

My best friend is my mum,
She is my best chum.
She is so good and kind,
She reads to me all the time.
My mum is a good cook,
She bought me my first cook book.
She makes great food to eat,
She gives us such a treat.
That's my mum, good and kind,
But she smells like rosemary wine.

Megan O'Neille (9)
Cranmore Integrated Primary School, Belfast

My Magic Box

(Based on 'Magic Box' by Kit Wright)

I will put in my box . . .
The juice of a crunchy apple I bit through,
The pips of my round, soft orange,
The spicy taste of the drippy Chinese sauce.

I will put in my box . . .
The warmness of a burning fire,
The happiness of the crazy parties,
The laughter at my funny jokes.

I will put in my box . . .
A fish that can breathe in the air,
A whale that can only breathe in water,
The worm that ruins plants.

My box is fashioned from light, sparkles and glitter,
With balls on the sides and stars on the top.

I shall go to a magical world with my box.

Leon Letzner Hawkins (8)
Cranmore Integrated Primary School, Belfast

The Weather

The seasons come in four:
Spring, summer, autumn and winter.
First we have the winter
When it's cold and harsh.
Next we have the lovely spring,
Full of new animals.
Third we have my favourite, the summer,
Full of the sun and lots of fun.
Then we have the golden autumn,
Conkers and leaves on the ground.
Then we start again,
Winter with the snow and Santa!

Lauren Allely (9)
Cranmore Integrated Primary School, Belfast

My Magic Box

(Based on 'Magic Box' by Kit Wright)

I will put in my box . . .
The cold winds of Donegal,
The frost of a winter's day,
The sunny days of summer.

I will put in my box . . .
A footballer with eight legs,
A spider playing football,
An everlasting gobstopper.

I will put in my box . . .
All the sweets in the world,
Ten million pounds,
One dog of every type.

My box is fashioned from
Cotton wool, steel and gold,
With the best guards in town.
It's as posh as a Bentley.

I shall sleep in it forever,
Until I die.
My box is fantastic.

Matthew McLean (9)
Cranmore Integrated Primary School, Belfast

The Person Who Wrote This

The person who wrote this poem
Is addicted to Lego,
Along with Star Wars
And also games consoles.
The things he hates mostly just food
And the things he likes mostly just toys.
And that's what the person who wrote this is like!

Adam Thomas-Mitchell (9)
Cranmore Integrated Primary School, Belfast

My Magic Box

(Based on 'Magic Box' by Kit Wright)

I will put in my box . . .
A freezing cold snowman,
A little puppy dog,
Soft snowdrops on your hand.

I will put in my box . . .
A bat with eight legs,
A spider with two wings,
A teacher with two heads.

I will put in my box . . .
Everlasting sweets,
Everlasting chocolate,
An everlasting mum.

My box is fashioned from gold and rubber
With squares on the lid.
Its lock is like a dinosaur's teeth.

I shall go swimming with my box in the sea,
Up a big wave and come back to
A big cup of hot chocolate.

Johna Crockett (9)
Cranmore Integrated Primary School, Belfast

Chocolate Poem

Chocolate is lovely,
Chocolate is nice,
Chocolate is tasty
In my tummy.
Chocolate is for everyone.
Chocolate I like the most.
Chocolate I scream and shout,
Chocolate I need you now!

Darren Milligan (9)
Cranmore Integrated Primary School, Belfast

My Magic Box
(Based on 'Magic Box' by Kit Wright)

I will put in my box . . .
My skateboard,
My family,
Going out with my friends.

I will put in my box . . .
Cleaners on a football pitch,
Footballers in the cleaners,
Man Utd.

I will put in my box . . .
My Nintendo
And my computer.

My box is made from
Water, rocks and stickers.

I shall drive my box
Round the race track
And come into the finish first.

Dylan Drain (8)
Cranmore Integrated Primary School, Belfast

A Victorian Child

Even on the coldest morns
I'm made to go out and work.
I start at five and end at eight,
I'd never dare to be late.

I get smacked and whipped
For the littlest wrong.
Factories of the Victorian age,
Phew, what a pong.

And when I'm finished
And finally go home,
Not allowed to see Mum or Dad,
It's as if I'm all alone.

Rachel McLean (11)
Cranmore Integrated Primary School, Belfast

My Magic Box

(Based on 'Magic Box' by Kit Wright)

I will put in my box . . .
A rose and petals from a buttercup,
The sound of flowers growing from the ground.

I will put in my magic box . . .
A good happy family
And an angry little tiger
And a sad little bear.

I will put in my magic box . . .
A sailing clown
And some little puppies.

I will put in my box . . .
Ice, gold and steel.

I will put in my box . . .
Memories of families.

I will put in my box . . .
Friends and pets.

Claire Kelly (8)
Cranmore Integrated Primary School, Belfast

Victorian Girl

It's 1853.
I'm as happy as can be.
Queen Victoria's on the throne,
So there is no need to moan.

I wear frilly dresses
So you can't make any messes.
Our servants are so lazy,
They drive me crazy.

There are people very ill,
So they can't work in Daddy's mill.
He says, 'Off to the workhouse they must go.'
But they shout, *'Oh no!'*

Louise Compston (11)
Cranmore Integrated Primary School, Belfast

My Magic Box

(Based on 'Magic Box' by Kit Wright)

I will put in my box . . .
The face of a seller,
The body of a footballer,
The voice of a singer.

I will put in my box . . .
The summer breeze,
The cold snow in the winter
And the birds singing in the spring.

I will put in my box . . .
Humans in the sea and fish walking on earth,
A man on Jupiter
And people on Mars.

My box is fashioned from diamonds
With a lid shaped like a square.
Its sides are made of money.

I shall surf on the moon
And on Earth beside my box.

Gavin Meehan (9)
Cranmore Integrated Primary School, Belfast

Little Match Girl

I'm sitting on the roadside,
Have not sold a single match,
I can't go home or Papa will beat me.
I'm very cold and my fingers are numb,
I light a match but I burn my finger.
I'm sleepy, echoes in my head
And I am very dizzy.
Slowly I lie down and fall
Into a deep, deep sleep
Which I will never be awoken from . . .

Hannah Murphy (10)
Cranmore Integrated Primary School, Belfast

My Magic Box

(Based on 'Magic Box' by Kit Wright)

I will put in my box . . .
A happy family,
A bunch of happy children,
A happy world.

I will put in my box . . .
The sound of someone dying,
The sound of a sad funeral.

I will put in my box . . .
My favourites: going on holiday,
Going on the computers,
Going on the school trips.

I will put in my box . . .
A dog in a man's bed
And a man in a dog's bed.

My box is fashioned from pink diamonds,
With nice baby-blue wallpaper.

Rachel Connolly (9)
Cranmore Integrated Primary School, Belfast

Hallowe'en Poem

H is for the horror
A is for the apple cake
L is for the lanterns
L is for the lifeless zombies
O is for October the 31st
W is for the wicked zombies
E is for the evil
E is for earning the candy
N is for night-time madness.

Conor Hanna (9)
Cranmore Integrated Primary School, Belfast

Wild Heart

Green grass all around,
Thumping hooves upon the ground,
Swishing tails of brown and black,
No leather saddle or man upon my back.
I have no heart that is tame,
All of us have stayed the same.

Black spots, white spots or blaze of white,
None of us lives in fright.
Wind rushing through our hair,
All our fur is as fair
As the snow that falls in the east.
People call us beasts.

Just because we're big,
We are not small like a fig,
Shetland, shire, chestnut, black,
None of us are turning back.
Stable master, boy or rider,
No, not us, we are the hiders.

We are the wild horses of the land,
Under hooves in the sand,
Wiry manes waving free,
Shiny like the crystal sea.
We are riding without glee,
We are free, can't you see?

Siva O'Neill (11)
Cranmore Integrated Primary School, Belfast

My Pet

My dragon's head is bigger than a T-rex.
His eyes glow like fire.
His teeth are sharp and massive.
His tail is larger than the sun.
His breath is stinking,
But I love him!

Rebecca Connolly (7)
Cranmore Integrated Primary School, Belfast

Life Is What You Make It

L ife is hard
I t has its ups and downs
F eeling happy and sad
E very day, month or year

I t's about being who you are
S aying what you feel

W ishing on dreams
H aving love shared
A ttending to people
T alking things through

Y ou should try to be happy
O r even sometimes sad
U nder your skin you can be beautiful

M ake up with friends
A lways try to say sorry
K indness is rewarding
E ven if you're not in the wrong

I t can be tough
T ake every day as it comes.

Jayne Nelson (10)
Cranmore Integrated Primary School, Belfast

Victorian Time

I am a little schoolboy,
Although I don't go to school,
And when I do I go for an hour in the afternoon.
When I'm not at school, I will be
Up a chimney brushing or sweeping it.
I get paid five pence a month.
I would rather to go school and play
Instead of up a chimney all day long!

Nicole Weir (11)
Cranmore Integrated Primary School, Belfast

My Kitten, Poppy

M is for mine because she is mine
Y is for young because she is young

K is for kitten because she's a kitten
I is for I love her
T is for too because she is too cute
T is for tiny because she is tiny
E is for energetic because she is energetic
N is for nosy because she is nosy

P is for Poppy because she is called Poppy
O is for only because she's the only cat I have
P is for pussy cat because she is a pussy cat
P is for ping-pong because she plays with ping-pong balls
Y is for yellow because she has a yellow collar.

Rhiannon Quinn-Nixon (10)
Cranmore Integrated Primary School, Belfast

My Magic Box

(Based on 'Magic Box' by Kit Wright)

I will put in my box . . .
My dog, Lucy,
My soft toy crocodile,
My robot dog called Texter.

I will put in my box . . .
Whenever I don't get to see my dog, Lucy,
And Andrew because he is my best friend.
Whenever I don't see my mum,
My TV and my favourite programme, Ed, Edd and Eddy.
And V-rex, the dinosaur.

I will put my Godzilla game
In my box.

Aaron Pollock (8)
Cranmore Integrated Primary School, Belfast

Victorians - Simply The Best!

One hundred and fifty years ago,
Queen Victoria reigned solo.
No electricity used for light,
Gas and candles helped with sight.
No cars or buses to get about,
Instead boats, trains or horses helped you out.
'Why are the Victorians so famous?' I hear you say,
That's because they ruled the day
And built an empire, huge and proud,
While other countries gasped out loud.
Factories and machines were made,
So lots of people were paid.
It was a time of tremendous change
Which people thought was very strange.
Instead of villages and working on the land,
Towns, shops and factories looked very grand.
Railways stretched from east to west.
Victorians were simply the best!

James Goldsmith (10)
Cranmore Integrated Primary School, Belfast

Gonna Throw Up

Giants puke on top of trees,
Pirates spew on stormy seas,
Dogs are sick in golden loos,
Kings throw up on people's shoes.

Boys like to make a mess
Down the front of Mum's best dress.
Roller coasters, swirling cups
Can make anyone throw up.

Sitting at the captain's table,
I scoffed as much as I was able.
I ate so many lovely fishes,
Ugh! Now it's time to clean the dishes.

Emma Ross (10)
Cranmore Integrated Primary School, Belfast

Introducing Me

Hi, it's Tom.
I'm fast and fun
On a football pitch.
I love to score and pass.
My dinner is always pasta.
I've got a sister and a brother,
I'm never bad.
Tidying up is what I hate to do.
Clever and cool,
That's me!

Thomas Earley (7)
Cranmore Integrated Primary School, Belfast

My Pet

My dragon's head is larger than a castle.
His eyes are red like the sun.
His teeth are sharp as knives.
His breath smells like rotting eggs.
His scales are rough like logs,
But he's a good friend to me!

Alysia Rea (7)
Cranmore Integrated Primary School, Belfast

My Pet

My dragon's head is larger than a hotel.
His eyes shine like blood.
His teeth are like sharp diamonds.
His breath is poisonous.
His spikes are pointy like horns,
But he's my super pet!

William Burke (7)
Cranmore Integrated Primary School, Belfast

Victorian Poem

I go to work.
The sun is not up yet.
My aching leg hurts.
I get beaten for arriving late.
I get started putting coal in the fire.
I get paid 2p a day
For twenty-two hours' work.
Back home I sleep in a small
Cold house, on the floor.
The life of a Victorian child.

Tom Polly (10)
Cranmore Integrated Primary School, Belfast

My Pet

My dragon's head is bigger than a house or school.
His eyes shine like rubies.
His teeth are sharper than a knife.
His pointy horns reach up to the mountains.
His breath stinks like vomit,
But he's cute!

Layna Morelli (7)
Cranmore Integrated Primary School, Belfast

My Pet

My dragon's head is larger than a flat.
His eyes shine bright like fire.
His scales are tougher than bricks.
His breath is smellier than rotting garbage.
His claws are strong like nails,
But he's my best pet!

Dillon Edgar-Lee (8)
Cranmore Integrated Primary School, Belfast

An Empty Child

After a night of shivering in an empty room,
The floor as your bed, a thin blanket as your duvet.
As you sadly walk to work, you think of happy times.
You are screamed at because you are thirty seconds late
Into the cold, wet, dangerous factory,
To thread things of wool together until your hands bleed,
Earn a mere 1 pence a day.
An orphan with a new family to cheer them up,
Working twenty-three hours a day with no breaks.
That is the life of a Victorian child.

Aoife Polly (10)
Cranmore Integrated Primary School, Belfast

My Pet

My dragon's head is larger than a flat.
His eyes shine brighter than the sun.
His scales are tougher than a mountain.
His breath is smellier than rotting garbage.
His claws cut through skin like razor blades,
But he's my best pet!

Matthew Sullivan (8)
Cranmore Integrated Primary School, Belfast

My Pet

My dragon's head is bigger than a hill.
His eyes shine yellow.
His claws are larger than a tornado.
His breath stinks like bloody snakes' eyeballs.
His massive tail crashes like a T-rex,
But he's good fun!

Zak Earley (7)
Cranmore Integrated Primary School, Belfast

The Chimney Boy

As the sun rises and the roses bloom
I am the chimney boy looking for chimneys to sweep.
I get five pence a day plus my face covered with soot
Because I'm not able to clean myself.
Walking from street, serving as many as possible.
My master takes care of me as best he can
So he can keep the house going from his pay and mine.
I am only eight and have a bleak future in front of me.

Stefan Angelone (10)
Cranmore Integrated Primary School, Belfast

The Victorian Life

A Victorian child could get very ill
Working in the workhouse or in a mill.
If they were good in school a wee bit
They wouldn't be humiliated by being beaten and hit.
Queen Victoria's family tree
Is good to learn in school for you and me.

Martin Kelley (10)
Cranmore Integrated Primary School, Belfast

Christmas

It's Christmas time again,
I'm feeling happy and excited.
I wonder if it's going to snow or rain.
I like to decorate the Christmas tree.
I like giving people Christmas presents
To show that I care about them.

Marie Toner (9)
Cranmore Integrated Primary School, Belfast

Victorian Poem

The Victorian times were cruel and mean,
They made the children sit in the corners and wear a dunce hat
And work from the age of five.
Adults only got paid if they worked overtime.
The Victorian people wore old-fashioned clothes
And the girls had to wear those things
That go round your waist to make you thin.

Chloe Hanna (10)
Cranmore Integrated Primary School, Belfast

Victorians

I'm a Victorian chimney sweep,
Up and down chimneys all day,
Nobody ever pays me and I never get to play.

I never get a rest
Because my master is a pest.
He makes me work in the rain,
He is such a pain.

Jack Creaner (10)
Cranmore Integrated Primary School, Belfast

An Autumn Poem

It was autumn,
The day was cold, crisp and clear.
The leaves were falling
Gently from the trees.
It made me very sad
Because the trees would not bloom
Until spring.

Gerard Loughran (9)
Cranmore Integrated Primary School, Belfast

Victorian Child

Up early in the morning,
I get dressed quickly
And off to work I go,
Sleepy and drowsy.
I carry a big, black, dirty brush.
Getting black already.
Climbing up chimneys
And sweeping them as
Clean as I can get them.
Hungry and tired,
But I still haven't finished my shift.
Finally, after a day's work
I can go home
And have dinner,
Put my feet up
And go to sleep.

Chloe Campbell (10)
Cranmore Integrated Primary School, Belfast

Popcorn

Popcorn, popcorn, 50p,
If you buy one, you get one free!
All the flavours you can smell,
Salted, sugar and sweet caramel.

Popcorn, popcorn, it's so good,
Popcorn, popcorn, it's my favourite food.

Ande Peden (10)
Cranmore Integrated Primary School, Belfast

Autumn

A pples fall off the trees
U mbrellas catch raindrops
T he animals hibernate for a long winter nap
U nderground moles hibernate
M onths are September, October and November
N ights are longer and colder.

Hayley Dodds (8)
Currie Primary School, Belfast

Autumn

A pples fall off the trees
U nderground animals hibernate
T he nights become longer
U mbrellas keep you dry from the rain
M oon is shining in the night sky
N uts fall off trees and squirrels take them.

Paul Robinson (7)
Currie Primary School, Belfast

Autumn

A pples fall off trees
U mbrellas keep the rain away
T rees lose their leaves
U pside down leaves hit the ground
M onths, there are three months in autumn
N ights are longer.

Dylan Johnston (7)
Currie Primary School, Belfast

Autumn

A pples are ready for eating
U p helicopters go, then land
T ea makes you warm
U nderground some animals hibernate
M unching squirrels
N ights turn darker.

Leon Glass (7)
Currie Primary School, Belfast

Autumn

A nimals hibernate
U p in the sky there goes a butterfly
T he days go colder
U mbrellas are used in autumn
M oon is low in autumn
N uts fall off a nut tree.

Britney Mason (7)
Currie Primary School, Belfast

Autumn

A nimals hibernate
U p in the sky is a moon
T he leaves fall off the trees
U mbrellas keep you dry
M oon is low
N ights are longer.

Cameron Ferris (7)
Currie Primary School, Belfast

Autumn

A nimals hibernate
U mbrellas block the rain
T he nights get colder and colder
U mbrellas get wet in autumn time
M oles live underground
N uts are on trees.

Brennan Sime (8)
Currie Primary School, Belfast

Chameleon - Haiku

Sitting on a tree,
Camouflaged against the branch,
Flicking its long tongue.

Adam Clyde (10)
Garryduff Primary School, Ballymoney

Anaconda - Haiku

Greenish chequered back
Hides from unsuspecting prey
In the shallow pool.

Andrew Young (11)
Garryduff Primary School, Ballymoney

Howler Monkey - Haiku

Eating bananas
Always looking for good food
Howling all day long.

Lucy Hassan (9)
Garryduff Primary School, Ballymoney

Gibbon - Haiku

Eating bananas
Coat black as a midnight sky
Hanging upside down.

Nicole Milliken (10)
Garryduff Primary School, Ballymoney

Python - Haiku

Coiled and motionless
Deadly power camouflaged
Awaiting its prey.

Lucy Buick (10)
Garryduff Primary School, Ballymoney

Morpho Butterfly - Haiku

Beautiful bright wings,
Fragile as fine gossamer,
Like a wisp of smoke.

Rebecca Macabe (10)
Garryduff Primary School, Ballymoney

Harpy Eagle - Haiku

Threat'ning, powerful,
Magnificent meat-eater,
Talons curved and long.

Peter Beattie (11)
Garryduff Primary School, Ballymoney

Autumn Is . . .

Autumn is . . .
    The sound of crispy leaves on the forest floor.
Autumn is . . .
    Shorter days and longer nights. *Great!* An extra hour in bed.
Autumn is . . .
    Sitting down to a lovely cup of hot chocolate.
Autumn is . . .
    Lying in front of a fire and watching television.
Autumn is . . .
    Having a scrumptious bowl of soup for me.
Autumn is . . .
    Soothing in a lovely warm bath.
Autumn soon will be over.

Adam Patrick (8)
Garryduff Primary School, Ballymoney

Jaguar - Haiku

A striped cat speeds past,
Disappears fast as lightning,
Feasts upon its prey.

Emma Hutchison (10)
Garryduff Primary School, Ballymoney

Autumn

Autumn is beautiful.
Leaves are falling off the trees like sprinkles going onto a cake.
Little birds are migrating to Ireland for their autumn holidays.
The cold, shivering animals are preparing for hibernation.
Our birds are migrating,
Flapping their wings across the ocean to reach their destiny.
Now harvest is here so now is the time to say
Thank you to God for all his wonderful blessings.

Andrew Hutchinson (9)
Garryduff Primary School, Ballymoney

Autumn

Autumn is a whirlwind of colour floating downwards.
Cups of hot chocolate and marshmallows
And a twirl of chocolate dripping down.
The sweet smell of fires on.
Cute ladybirds sadly dying.
Juicy, delicious, ripe berries growing on trees.
Burning hot bonfires, flames going high up in the sky.
Beautiful, rosy-coloured, poor dying flowers.
Joyful singing of migrating birds.
Fabulous, mythical autumn!

Stephanie Love (8)
Garryduff Primary School, Ballymoney

Tiger - Haiku

Orange eyes of fire
Pierce the uproar of the night,
Glow of orange strikes!

Jenny Love (10)
Garryduff Primary School, Ballymoney

Autumn

Cold, crispy days lingering like delicate icicles.
Leaves whirling like a tornado around my head.
Leaves falling like drops of rain out of the sky.
Birds' wings flutter like leaves from a tree.
Birds pecking at berries like woodpeckers at a tree.
Green grass frosted with shadows of white,
Changing it overnight.
Mystical, mysterious autumn.

Jack McMullan (9)
Garryduff Primary School, Ballymoney

Autumn

Autumn is colourful,
Beautiful leaves floating down like snow.
Trees frozen with ice crystals on them.
In my house I love to sit by the roasting, warm, cosy fire,
With a cup of hot milk and brown chocolate,
With Smarties and sprinkles.
Scary costumes at Hallowe'en,
With their juicy, sweet, tasty, yummy sweets.
It's prize day at Sunday school.
I can't wait to buy something playful!

Elizabeth Gaston (8)
Garryduff Primary School, Ballymoney

Parakeet - Haiku

Loudly calling out,
Dazzling the air with colour
As it swoops to land.

Charlotte Calderwood (10)
Garryduff Primary School, Ballymoney

Toucan - Haiku

Beautiful colours,
Rainbow of clouds floating low,
What a lovely sight!

Lucy Gaston (10)
Garryduff Primary School, Ballymoney

Tarantula - Haiku

Softly scuffling on
Through the darkened forest floor
For its tasty feast!

Justine McNougher (11)
Garryduff Primary School, Ballymoney

Crazy Pets

I have loads of pets,
Big ones, small ones,
Fat and thin.

I have a hamster,
He is brown, white and dark black,
His name is Fidget.

I have two dogs,
Their names are Muttly and Mo.
They just love to play.

I have sixteen hens
And a brown leghorn rooster.
They all love their maize.

Alison Gamble (10)
Kingsmills Primary School, Armagh

Conkers - Cinquain

Conkers
Falling from trees
Cracking, making them free
In its spiky case it is hard
Fighting.

Ryan Walker (10)
Kingsmills Primary School, Armagh

Exploding - Cinquain

Fireworks
Bright, colourful,
Exploding bright up high,
Colours right up high in the sky,
Lovely.

Deborah King (10)
Kingsmills Primary School, Armagh

Ponies - Haikus

Ponies can gallop
And a pony can canter,
A pony can walk.

Ponies need their tack
With brushes, combs and saddle
And a nice holder.

Ponies' colours are
Black, white, brown, grey and spotty,
Like a fast cheetah.

Danielle Hazley (8)
Kingsmills Primary School, Armagh

Christmas - Cinquain

Christmas,
Santa has come,
He has got children toys.
Wish the children have a good day.
Snowfall.

Robert Ferris (8)
Kingsmills Primary School, Armagh

Christmas - Cinquain

Christmas,
Money, presents,
Christmas tree lights on trees,
On Christmas Day there is snowfall,
Rudolph.

Alistair Marks (10)
Kingsmills Primary School, Armagh

Goldfish - Haikus

There was a small fish
Flakes were his favourite dish
He had a castle

One day he played tricks
He pretended to be sick
The owner helped him

He found a buddy
Her new nickname is Ruddy
They both play all day

They love the water
Now they have a small daughter
They truly love her.

David Cartmill (10)
Kingsmills Primary School, Armagh

Spooky - Cinquain

Spooky,
Hallowe'en night
Scary masks and faces
Trick or treat, getting our candy,
Scary.

Amy Cartmill (10)
Kingsmills Primary School, Armagh

Christmas - Cinquain

Christmas,
Elves make the toys,
Santa comes at night-time,
All the snow is fun to play in,
Have fun.

Killian Walker (9)
Kingsmills Primary School, Armagh

Farm Animals - Haikus

My sheep are quite fat
They are frightened of a bat
They are very cute

I love white strong cows
I wish I had a stout sow
My hens are scarlet

I have a black cat
Its best-loved food is a rat
Goats make creamy milk

My friend has a duck
A boy goat is called a buck
Horses are pretty.

Kyle Rogers (9)
Kingsmills Primary School, Armagh

Rabbit Crazy - Haikus

Buggsy, my rabbit
Is black and white, he is Dutch.
He has a pine hutch.

My cute rabbit plays
Outside in his long, long run
Where he shades from sun.

Buggsy is happy,
He's always in a good mood
When he gets his food.

Buggsy likes to play
In his favourite fawn hutch.
I love him so much.

Hannah Brady (11)
Kingsmills Primary School, Armagh

Run Away Quick - Haikus

I eat some toffee
People always give the spooks
I like to read books.

Running loose is good.
Trick or treating is the best.
I forget the rest.

Eating sweets and buns.
Walking home that night I think,
Is the toffee pink?

Pop, crackle and snap
Goes the bonfire really loud.
It is a big cloud.

Some marshmallows melt.
It is a good Hallowe'en.
What have I just seen?

Adam Copeland (10)
Kingsmills Primary School, Armagh

Seasons - Haikus

All about seasons,
Bright, colourful things around,
Leaves fall to the ground.

Green, brown, red, orange,
These are the colours you see,
Look, a buzzing bee.

Hot, cold, windy, rain,
Autumn, winter, summer, spring,
Summertime birds sing.

Woolly hats, scarves, boots,
Snow falls down like cotton buds,
Clouds are bathtub suds.

Lucy Bell (11)
Kingsmills Primary School, Armagh

Pets - Haikus

I have got a dog,
I like to play fetch with her.
Her name is Gemma.

My rabbit, Buggsy,
Is very, very fluffy,
Like a fur teddy.

If I had a cat
I would play with it all day
With my friend, Dannielle.

If I had a bird
It would fly about the day
And come back at night.

Nicole Brady (8)
Kingsmills Primary School, Armagh

Birds

Birds are having chicks,
Eggs are hatching in their nests,
Then they fly away.

Chicks are being fed,
Bird tables are being built,
Chicks are chirping now.

Birds sing very nicely,
Today they sing happily
And they sound the same.

Andrew Hamilton (8)
Kingsmills Primary School, Armagh

Christmas - Cinquain

Christmas,
Fun and presents
Running, laughing, singing,
Getting presents from Santa Claus,
Presents.

Thomas Ferris (10)
Kingsmills Primary School, Armagh

Anger

Anger is red like a fire.
It sounds like monsters in the night.
It tastes like cheese.
It smells like revenge.
It feels like it's the end of the world.
It looks like your face is all crumpled.
It reminds you of life - how it used to be.

Lesley Thompson (11)
Maghaberry Primary School, Craigavon

Blackbird

I like shiny stuff,
Gold, diamond rings
And all kinds of things.

People phone the police,
But they cannot see
That it is mostly me.

I have a lot of stuff
Because I am the best,
So I need a big nest.

Nathan Harper (9)
Maghaberry Primary School, Craigavon

Angelfish

I am an angelfish,
As posh as posh can be.
My lovely large home
Is in the middle of the sea.

I've got colourful scales,
Fluorescent green, yellow and pink.
The others say I'm beautiful,
I always make them wink.

I don't think I'm beautiful,
But gorgeous, fantastic,
And all the other dumbo fish
Look like they're made out of plastic.

I am just so gorgeous,
I can't help knowing that,
It's a gift that I was given,
I'm definitely not fat.

Catherine Courtney (10)
Maghaberry Primary School, Craigavon

Lonely Panda

Mostly I'm in trees looking for bamboo
And I'm very lonely, nobody plays with me,
Maybe I'm not good enough.
Will you play with me?

I have a hard life,
Other pandas steal my bamboo,
And then I just say boohoo.
Hunters try to shoot me.

It's just for my fur,
So please help me.
Please give me a real rainforest home,
A real place I can call home.

Ross Curry (10)
Maghaberry Primary School, Craigavon

Monkey

I am a monkey,
I play all day long,
Swinging on trees
And singing a song.

I balance with my tail,
Sometimes I fall,
But I am so silly,
I don't care at all.

I love bananas,
I eat them with a squash,
But sometimes I get them all over myself,
And I have to have a wash.

I am a monkey,
The silliest one.
My friends say I'm stupid,
But I do it for fun.

Kyle Hayes (10)
Maghaberry Primary School, Craigavon

Panda

I live in the zoo,
I eat bamboo
And play with my friends.

I'm five years old
But I look so old,
Sunbathing all day!

My best friends are bears,
They like to eat pears
And why? I haven't a clue!

I go for a run,
Then bathe in the sun
On lovely warm days!

Amy Jennings (9)
Maghaberry Primary School, Craigavon

Silence

Silence is dark like walking in a deserted graveyard on your own.
It feels as if goosebumps are crawling up your spine like the
ghost of death.
It reminds me of the day I found out I was deaf, that dark,
gloomy day.
It tastes like chewing a fork but doesn't make a sound.
It smells like a smoky classroom on your own.
It sounds like a road with no traffic on it.
Silence reminds me of all these things when it's around.

Clara Dawson (10)
Maghaberry Primary School, Craigavon

Darkness

Darkness is as black as thick black smoke from a huge fire.
Darkness feels like an ice shower in a paper bath.
Darkness reminds me of an uncomforting shadow, forever following.
Darkness tastes like overly sugared tea.
Darkness sounds like an unusual tapping.
Darkness looks like a winter's night sky.
Darkness smells like petrol on a cold morning.

Megan Haste (10)
Maghaberry Primary School, Craigavon

Laughter

Laughter is like the joy in my heart.
Laughter reminds me of jokes on April Fools Day.
Laughter tastes like chocolate melting in my mouth.
Laughter feels soft and fluffy like the slippers on my feet.
Laughter smells like freshly cut grass that we play on.
Laughter is multicoloured like the rainbow flying high in the sky.
Laughter sounds like music to my ears.

Jack Wilson (10)
Maghaberry Primary School, Craigavon

Hunger

Hunger is grey like the colour of iron bars blocking the fridge.
Hunger tastes like a dry, rough desert in my mouth.
Hunger sounds like a rumbling child's stomach.
Hunger reminds me of less fortunate children who have nothing
                                                    to eat.
Hunger looks like a sweet shop without sweets.
Hunger feels like emptiness in my stomach.
Hunger smells like melted chocolate that you're running towards
                                        but you never reach it.

Katherine Madden (11)
Maghaberry Primary School, Craigavon

Silence

Silence is white like the fluffy clouds in the light blue sky.
Silence feels like my soft fluffy pillow on my soft warm bed.
Silence tastes like dark chocolate ice cream from a Ben & Jerry's tub.
Silence reminds me of the world as it was clean.
Silence looks like snow twinkling down onto the black gleaming road.
Silence sounds like birds singing their lungs out with joy on the
                                        tallest trees.
Silence smells like the fresh air in a luscious green field.

Emma Saulters (10)
Maghaberry Primary School, Craigavon

Silence

Silence is white like the bright, bright sun.
Silence is like a dark empty cemetery on a cold stormy night.
Silence is like a relaxing, peaceful nothingness.
Silence feels like calming water running down your neck.
Silence tastes like a relaxing hot drink on a cold winter's day.
Silence reminds me of a waterfall gently flowing into a stream.
Silence feels like a wet blanket gently set on your face.

Garrett Dalcz (10)
Maghaberry Primary School, Craigavon

Happiness

Happiness is red like an apple.
Happiness sounds like teeth crunching.
It tastes like jam on toast.
It smells like chewing gum.
It feels like a soft pillow.
It looks like a heart pumping up and down.
It reminds me of someone sharing and being kind.

Sarah Bradford (10)
Maghaberry Primary School, Craigavon

Laughter

Laughter is like green for joy.
Laughter is like someone being happy.
Laughter is like someone smiling.
Laughter is like someone going to the zoo.
Laughter feels bouncy and soft.
Laughter tastes like sweets that never dissolve.
Laughter reminds me of Christmas Day!

Nicola Wright (10)
Maghaberry Primary School, Craigavon

Hunger

Hunger is black like an empty boot.
Hunger sounds like agony.
Hunger looks like an empty fruit bowl.
Hunger smells like a burning fire.
Hunger tastes like ashes.
Hunger feels like being trapped.
Hunger reminds me of dry fruit.

Ross McLernon (10)
Maghaberry Primary School, Craigavon

Silence

Silence is red like a burning forest fire.
Silence tastes like roast potatoes.
Silence sounds like wind blowing in my ear.
Silence looks like an empty book.
Silence feels like the sea air.
Silence smells like milk.
Silence reminds me of being frightened.

Jordan Jack (11)
Maghaberry Primary School, Craigavon

Fear

Fear is yellow like a lemon.
It sounds like bass drums battering in my ear.
It tastes like worms in my mouth.
It smells like a fear that I'm scared of.
It feels like slimy things.
It looks like something you are scared of.
It reminds me of not being scared.

Aaron Houston (10)
Maghaberry Primary School, Craigavon

Love

Love is pink like a thumping heart.
It sounds like a soft melody.
It tastes like melted chocolate.
It smells like bright red roses.
It feels like a bunny rabbit.
It looks like a western sunset.
It reminds me of my family and me.

Zoe McAllister (11)
Maghaberry Primary School, Craigavon

Hunger

Hunger is black like an empty stomach begging for food.
Hunger feels terrible, it's standing in the desert with no hope of
getting home.
Hunger sounds rainy like bullets coming out of a gun.
Hunger smells like death and rotten food.
Hunger tastes like nothing, only air.
Hunger looks like skinny children, like bags of bones.
Hunger reminds me of the poor African children, as poor as a tree.

Jonathan Murray (10)
Maghaberry Primary School, Craigavon

Fun

Fun is orangey-yellow like a hot and sandy beach.
Fun feels like swaying grass, silky and smooth.
Fun tastes like an ice cream slowly dripping on your tongue.
Fun looks like a wide green meadow filled with pansies and roses.
Fun sounds like a roaring sea where the dolphins sing their song.
Fun smells like a great aroma leaking from the flowers.
Fun reminds me of holidays when freedom lurks in the air.

Joshua Moffett (11)
Maghaberry Primary School, Craigavon

Laughter

Laughter is red like a red light glowing in the dark.
Laughter sounds crazy like someone going made in their house.
Laughter tastes warm like a hot doughnut being eaten in a café.
Laughter feels tickly, like a feather brushing against my arm.
Laughter reminds me of fun, like going down a slide.
Laughter smells like hot dogs and warm sausages.

Adam Spence (10)
Maghaberry Primary School, Craigavon

Excitement!

Excitement is like fluorescent yellow.
It sounds like loud girly screams.
It tastes like something is alive in your mouth, wiggling like crazy.
It smells like a zillion bits of pollen have gone up your nose when
sniffing a flower.
It feels like a massage chair going one hundred times faster
than fast.
It looks like a storm of buzzing bees going extremely speedily in
and out.
It reminds me of when I can't wait and it is impossible to be patient.

Adam Smylie (10)
Maghaberry Primary School, Craigavon

Fun

Fun is blue and orange like the warm sky when you're playing
happily outside.
Fun looks like everybody playing together in the sun.
Fun tastes like candy formed into chocolate sponge.
Fun sounds like love in your heart, thumping.
Fun reminds me of friends and family on Christmas Day.
Fun feels like chocolate cake, fudge and ice cream melting on
my tongue.

Melissa Martin (10)
Maghaberry Primary School, Craigavon

Excitement!

Excitement is the colour yellow because yellow is bright.
It sounds like magic is everywhere.
It tastes sour and makes your taste buds jump.
It smells like pure chocolate melted.
It feels jumpy and crazy and wiggly.
It looks like people dancing in the moonlight.
It reminds me of people having fun and going *crazy!*

Abby Eagleson (10)
Maghaberry Primary School, Craigavon

Excitement

Excitement is red like an apple.
It sounds like screams from a speeding roller coaster.
It tastes like candyfloss from a theme park.
It smells like fresh air.
It feels like you're being tickled.
It looks like a person flying down from a Hurricane Condor.
It reminds me of going on my first roller coaster.

Christopher Clulow (10)
Maghaberry Primary School, Craigavon

Fear

Fear is black like the lingering darkness of the night.
It sounds like a million bugs crawling all over you.
It tastes like mushy carrot in your mouth.
It smells like a cold and damp, sweaty coat.
It feels like it makes your skin tingle.
It looks like the most terrifying creature from space
And it reminds me of a nightmare.

Kyle Minford (10)
Maghaberry Primary School, Craigavon

Sadness

Sadness is blue like a river.
It sounds like tears dripping off someone's face.
It tastes bitter like a lemon.
It smells like an onion.
It feels like everyone is against you.
It looks like death.
It reminds me of my grandad who died.

Megan Armstrong (11)
Maghaberry Primary School, Craigavon

Anger

Anger is the colour red like a tomato.
Anger sounds like drums beating in my head.
Anger tastes like a bitter taste and mucus.
Anger smells like bad, horrid, disgusting decay.
Anger feels like bad and horrid.
Anger looks like redness - ugly.
Anger reminds me of badness, jealousy and hatred.

Harriet Kelso (10)
Maghaberry Primary School, Craigavon

Anger

Anger is red like a fire.
It crackles like a fire as well.
It tastes like blood in my mouth.
It smells like smoke from a wood fire.
It feels like a thousand pins pricking me inside.
It looks like the thing you hate most.
It reminds me of my brother shouting in my ear.

Hannah McConnell (10)
Maghaberry Primary School, Craigavon

Fun

Fun looks like a magical rainbow.
Fun sounds like a whole new world.
Fun tastes as if it never wants to go.
It smells as if it lives here.
It feels like a cotton cloud filled with marshmallows.
It looks like freedom has just begun.
It reminds me of a beautiful, loving world.

Shannon Elliott (10)
Maghaberry Primary School, Craigavon

Hatred

Hatred is dark and damp.
It sounds like cries and moans.
It tastes like sour, bitter lemon
And smells like rotting fish.
Hatred feels like ragged barbed wire
And looks like a black broken heart
With an arrow shot halfway through it.
Hatred reminds me of sadness in my heart.

Jonathan Good (11)
Maghaberry Primary School, Craigavon

My Hallowe'en Poem

Hallowe'en, Hallowe'en, it's here at last.
Scary creatures and ghosts come back from the past.
Haunted house rattles at night.
Hallowe'en, Hallowe'en, fireworks and bonfires.
Sweets and candy is all our desire.
Hallowe'en, Hallowe'en is over with a blast,
We all must go to bed because it's half-past.

Conor Reilly (9)
Our Lady's & St Mochua's Primary School, Derrynoose

My Dog, Jane

My dog, Jane, licks me on the face
When she is happy.
She scratches the back door,
Wanting inside.
She lets me skip
Without biting the rope.

Catherine McGuigan (8)
Our Lady's & St Mochua's Primary School, Derrynoose

Genie

I am a genie from afar,
I'll grant you a wish for a chocolate bar.
If it's not nice,
You'll pay the price,
I'll feed you to the dreaded mice.
I am a genie from afar,
Don't upset me, I know where you are.

Jennifer Lynch (10)
Our Lady's & St Mochua's Primary School, Derrynoose

My Dog, Snoopy

S pots remind me of my little dog
N oisy is his thing
O nce he bit my sandal
O pen his eyes, there will be a surprise
P awprints are everywhere
Y our nose is everywhere, and your smile.

Rebecca McNaughton (8)
Our Lady's & St Mochua's Primary School, Derrynoose

Dogs

Some are cute,
Some are big and like to fetch twigs.
Some are funny and very jumpy,
Some are very thin.
Some are very fat and very playful.
I like brown and white puppies,
Ones that like to play fetch.

Emily Hannify (8)
Our Lady's & St Mochua's Primary School, Derrynoose

Dogs And Puppies

Dogs are cute,
Puppies are sweet,
Every day they lick my feet.
They eat,
They bite,
They love to use their sight.
They run,
They jump,
They play dead,
They bark, they sniff,
They sleep on the bed.

Erin McGinnity (9)
Our Lady's & St Mochua's Primary School, Derrynoose

Aaron

A aron is fantastic
A mazing at sport
R ough and tumble, still survives
O n the go all the time
N ever lets you down

F abulous at not keeping quiet
O nly great to his friend
X -Factor he wishes to win, but then again he's in a bin!

Aaron Fox (10)
Our Lady's & St Mochua's Primary School, Derrynoose

Mary

M ary is my name
A aron is my best, best friend
R ock and roll is my thing
Y ou are my best friend, Aaron.

Mary Callaghan (8)
Our Lady's & St Mochua's Primary School, Derrynoose

I Love School

I love school,
It's so cool.
We have art every day,
We love to play.
I love school,
It's so cool.
I know you love school,
It loves you too.
I love school,
It's so cool.
We love school!

Ciara Mallon (9)
Our Lady's & St Mochua's Primary School, Derrynoose

Dan Shanahan

Dan the man,
He really can
Make you spin like a fan.
What a hurler,
What a man,
He really is
Super Dan!

Peter McKearney (11)
Our Lady's & St Mochua's Primary School, Derrynoose

Mint, My Real Dog!

M int is my marvellous dog
 I n an incredible world
N othing less than cute
 T ackles my daddy's boot!

Orla Breen (11)
Our Lady's & St Mochua's Primary School, Derrynoose

Cats

Some cats are
Fat and fluffy,
Some cats are thin,
Some cats don't
Have fur,
Only pinky skin.
Some are cute,
Others are funny,
I've got one of those,
I call her Sunny.
Sunny will make me happy
When I'm sad,
So I am glad
That I've got a friendly cat
Like Sunny.
It was worth the money.

Emma-Kate Haughey (9)
Our Lady's & St Mochua's Primary School, Derrynoose

My Baby Cousin

My baby cousin,
He is so cute.
My baby cousin,
He smiles when I play the flute.

My baby cousin,
He likes clowns.
My baby cousin,
He hates loud sounds.

My baby cousin,
Let's go play with Rover.
My baby cousin,
The day is over.

Carolyn Fitzpatrick (9)
Our Lady's & St Mochua's Primary School, Derrynoose

Teacher, Teacher

Teacher, Teacher,
It's not fair,
Cormac pulled
Dina's hair,
Now she's crying
In the loo,
So I came
Straight to you.
Teacher, Teacher
It's not fair,
Liam ripped
Erin's bear.
Erin thinks
I'm to blame
So I come
To you again!
Teacher, Teacher,
It's not fair,
Pearse has broken
Emma's chair,
Then he spilt
The pencil pot
And made Mary
Clean the lot.
Teacher, Teacher,
This is bad!
All the children
Must be mad!
Teacher, Teacher,
Please don't shout,
Give us a minute
To sort it out!

Alice Lennon (9)
Our Lady's & St Mochua's Primary School, Derrynoose

My Cat

I love my cat very dearly

L ily is my cat's kitten
O ver the moon is my cat when she sees me coming
V ery cute is my cat
E very evening she waits by my doorstep

Y asmine is my cat's name
A very good cat that's mine
S almon and tuna is my cat's favourite meal
M y cat is the best, better than all the rest
I know my cat's a good mouse-catcher
N ever, ever will she scrab
E very day she is so good that I have to give her extra food.

Catherine Nugent (9)
Our Lady's & St Mochua's Primary School, Derrynoose

My Tractor

I stare out at her
Shiny red body in the rain.
The rain drops down on her nose.
Her eyes flash at me.

She helps me catch the cows on the farm.
She races up and down the lane.
She takes me up to the house
When I am sleepy from my work.

When I feed her she spins her wheel
In a sign of happiness.
Me and my tractor are like
The best of friends.

Gabrielle Fox (9)
Our Lady's & St Mochua's Primary School, Derrynoose

My Dog, Fightin

A gentle autumn breeze
Sweeps through my hair
As I walk through the park,
I breathe in the air.
My life will always be exciting
Cos he's here, my dog, Fightin.

His life is good,
Just as it should,
If I was like that
It would drive me bonkers.
He does nothing wrong,
He collects conkers,
Cos he's here, my dog, Fightin.

What a good sight,
It would give you a fright,
He wouldn't care if there's blight -
He'd eat anything
And all he wants is a fight!

Michael McGrane (11)
Our Lady's & St Mochua's Primary School, Derrynoose

Heidi

My cat's called Heidi,
Oh what a sight!

She sleeps on my silk nightie,
Eating food to her delight.

She's rather a snob,
But that's her job,

Sleeping by the stove,
That's my sweet love.

Olivia McKearney (10)
Our Lady's & St Mochua's Primary School, Derrynoose

A Recipe To Turn Teachers Into Spiders

Take one snake, soak in slime,
Gently drip slugs and bugs into grime,
Add the promise of Teacher's heart
To turn it into an apple tart.

Season with crunched snakeskin
And the sound of the school's wheelie bin.

Mix in bones and groans and some stories of ghosts and ghouls,
And some of the teachers' working tools.

Finally add some cheesy Cheddar,
Then watch and your teacher will turn into
A spider.

Shannon McGuigan (10)
Our Lady's & St Mochua's Primary School, Derrynoose

Hair

Hair, hair,
You can have fair,
Fair like mine,
Or blonde if you're fond.

Some like short,
Some like long,
So they can use
The curling tong.

Hair can be up or down,
Bobbed or spiked,
But the funniest of all is my dad's,
Because he is bald.

Keelin Boyd (10)
Our Lady's & St Mochua's Primary School, Derrynoose

My Cat, Scratchy

My cat, Scratchy, loves to eat,
Especially when I give her treats.
She looks for food every day,
So why not give her some and play?
My cat, Scratchy, loves her food.

My cat, Scratchy, loves to play,
She waits for me every day.
She runs about and catches mice,
She's a lovely cat, so very nice.

My cat, Scratchy, is just like me,
Soft and cuddly as can be.
My cat, Scratchy, my best friend,
I'll love her always,
To the end.

Ellen Hamilton (9)
Our Lady's & St Mochua's Primary School, Derrynoose

Me

I don't like to brag,
But I am the best!
I am good at tag,
Better than all the rest!
I don't like school,
I am very cool . . .
I am pretty
Like my cat, Metty.
I cam cool, can't you see?
This poem is just about me!

Hannah Finnegan (10)
Our Lady's & St Mochua's Primary School, Derrynoose

My Parents

M y parents are best, that is all I have to say
Y ou may not believe it, but it's true

P arents are the best things in the world, but mine are the best
A ll they do is love me to bits
R eally all my parents want to do is be the best parents ever, but
they already are

E veryone loves my parents, but I love them the most
N ow do you believe me that I have the best parents in the world?
T hey may be silly at times, but they are mine
S ome people say they have got the best parents, but I have them
right here.

Marie-Claire Burke (10)
Our Lady's & St Mochua's Primary School, Derrynoose

Peter

My friend is Peter,
He's a pizza eater,
He's well over a metre,
He plays for Derrynoose,
He's an all star on the loose,
And that's my friend, Peter.

Ryan Murray (11)
Our Lady's & St Mochua's Primary School, Derrynoose

Lady

L oveliest dog in the world
A ctive, bouncy, lively
D ays we spent together
Y ears we spent together

We miss you, Lady.

Eryn Murphy (9)
Our Lady's & St Mochua's Primary School, Derrynoose

Dogs

Dogs, dogs, have a good fight,
They also have a very big bite.

Every time they fight,
They always have a might.
Everyone loves dogs, they're always a sight.

They love delight,
Like a little kite.

The pups are so cute,
They're as cute as a brute.

Peter Parker (10)
Our Lady's & St Mochua's Primary School, Derrynoose

Astronaut Or Clown?

An astronaut goes into space,
Forgets to tie a space bootlace,
Runs on the moon at his best pace,
Lo and behold, falls on his face.
Hurts his head,
Ends up dead,
Should have been a clown instead.

Kevin McKenna (10)
Our Lady's & St Mochua's Primary School, Derrynoose

Christmas

Christmas, Christmas is such a joy,
Santa comes and you get a toy!
You might also get a delight
When Santa comes at night.
Leave out a carrot and maybe some sweets,
Who knows what treats you might receive?
You might get the things you asked for as well,
But it's the big surprise that goes down well.

Sinead McKee (10)
Our Lady's & St Mochua's Primary School, Derrynoose

Last

I like to play sports,
I like to run fast,
Last time, I ran too fast.
Ended up in a hard cast.
That was the last,
The last of the last!
The last time I'll ever come last!

Ciara Woods (10)
Our Lady's & St Mochua's Primary School, Derrynoose

Shoes

Shoes, shoes,
Which ones should I choose?
From sandals to flip-flops,
From stilettos to boots,
All of the things that my feet suit.

Which ones should I buy?
Which ones should I wear?
Which will suit my outfit?
Ah, those ones over there!

Amanda Tomany (11)
Our Lady's & St Mochua's Primary School, Derrynoose

My Pony

My pony is called Chocolate,
It is a brown pony.
It has long brown hair
And it has pink ribbons too.
It can run and jump and swim,
But best of all, I can ride it too.

Juliette Roberts (7)
Portadown Integrated Primary School, Portadown

My Teacher

My teacher is sweet
She is nice
She is the best
She is fun

My teacher is beautiful
She is pretty
She is perfect
She is clever

My teacher is sweet
My teacher is beautiful
She is nice
She is pretty

My teacher is perfect.

Abigail Uprichard (8)
Portadown Integrated Primary School, Portadown

My Mad Teacher

I think my teacher must have gone mad,
She let us out of school at twelve
When we usually get out at three.
She didn't give us any homework today.
She made us play all day and I loved it.
Our teacher gave us sweets to eat today,
Then she made us go home and watch TV.
Ring, ring, ring, ring goes the alarm.
Oh no . . . it was all a dream.

Caoimhe Cullen (8)
Portadown Integrated Primary School, Portadown

His Last Chance

His last chance,
Caged,
Lonely,
As the little lion cries.

His last chance,
His ears
Drooping,
As the little lion hides.

His last chance,
His nose
Dry,
As the little lion lies.

His last chance,
His eyes
Sorrowful,
As the little lion sleeps, heartbroken.

His last chance,
Caged,
Lonely,
As he cries . . . cries . . . cries . . .

Aidan Cairns (10)
Portadown Integrated Primary School, Portadown

Fairies

I love fairies
And I look out of the window
To see a group of fairies,
But I haven't seen a fairy yet.
One day I saw a fairy
And the next day was a fairy day.
Mum said, 'I don't believe in fairies.'
Dad said, 'You are such a little dreamer.'
But I know that *fairies are real.*

Hallie Adams (8)
Portadown Integrated Primary School, Portadown

Past Her Prime

Past her prime,
Enclosed,
Isolated,
The grey wolf paces.

Past her prime,
Her tail
Loops,
The grey wolf howls.

Past her prime,
Her eyes
Cry,
The grey wolf hides.

Past her prime,
Her fur
Tatty,
The grey wolf sleeps.

Past her prime,
Enclosed,
Isolated,
The grey wolf paces . . . paces . . . paces lonely.

Jessica Alexander (10)
Portadown Integrated Primary School, Portadown

Words Are Important!

Words are very important things,
Words can make you feel happy,
Words can make you sad,
Words can make you full of glee,
Words can make you feel bad.
Be careful how you use your words,
Think before you speak.
Some words that you think are fun
Could actually be full of cheek.

Cliodhna Morgan (9)
Portadown Integrated Primary School, Portadown

What Has Happened to Matthew?

(Based on 'What Has Happened to Lulu?' by Charles Causley)

What has happened to Matthew, Mother?
What has happened to Matt?
There's nothing in his bed but an old Arsenal top,
And by its side a hurling bat.

Why is his door open wide, Mother?
His boots on the floor
And only two circles on his dusty table
Where his football was there before?

Why do you look so sad, Mother,
And why does your bottom lip shake?
Andy why do you put that letter in the bin
And say it's nothing but a fake?

I woke to noises late last night,
I heard the engine sound.
Why do you tell me the sounds that I hear
Were a dream that my mind found?

I heard somebody in tears, Mother,
In temper or in agony.
Now I question you why, Mother?
You say it was only the sea.

Why did you wander in front of the fire
Where you miserably sat?
What has happened to Matthew, Mother?
What has happened to Matt?

Niall Magee (10)
Portadown Integrated Primary School, Portadown

What Happened To Keelan?

(Based on 'What Has Happened to Lulu?' by Charles Causley)

What happened to Keelan, Mother?
What happened to Keely?
There's nothing left in his nice little hut,
Except a picture of Makele.

Why is his wardrobe open wide, Mother?
With water flowing free
And only a mark on the dusty floor
Where his football boots used to be.

Why do you look so sad, Mother,
With tears falling out of your eyes?
And why don't you tell me the truth
Instead of all these lies?

I woke to noises late last night,
I heard an engine roar.
Why did I hear the noises
When I woke up from my snore?

I heard someone crying, Mother,
In anger or in pain,
But why do you tell me now, Mother,
That it's just the stupid rain?

Why do you wander around
Like you don't know what to do?
What has happened to Keelan, Mother?
What happened to Keely?

Cian Murtagh (9)
Portadown Integrated Primary School, Portadown

What Makes Me Smile!

My mum makes me smile
When she tells a funny joke.
My granny makes me smile
When she can't work the remote.

My grandpa makes me smile
When he takes me out with the dog.
My cousins make me smile
When they take me over to the bog.

My sister makes me smile
When she's not fighting with me.
My auntie makes me smile
When she tries to climb a tree.

Mr Gordon makes me smile
When he praises my work.
My friends make me smile
When they scribble with the chalk.

Julia Camporese (10)
Portadown Integrated Primary School, Portadown

Christmas

Santa Claus, Santa Claus,
With a sack full of toys,
Don't bring anything
For the naughty boys.

Santa Claus, Santa Claus,
With the sack the size of your belly,
I'm still watching
The telly.

Santa Claus, Santa Claus,
With a suit so red,
When you come down my chimney,
Your suit will be black and I'll be in bed.

Nadine McNally (9)
Portadown Integrated Primary School, Portadown

Eww, Gross

Look into my brother's bedroom,
You will be very surprised,
Though you think it's slimy gunk,
It really is just smelly junk!

Well you should see his bunk beds,
They both are such a mess,
And what's in his bedside table drawer?
Mouldy sandwiches, you might guess.

Wow, look at that wardrobe!
It is such a tip.
I'm telling you it's revolting.
Every time Mum walks in she nearly flips.

Well there you go, that's my bro's room,
I'm sure you don't want to stay.
Maybe you should come on round
And check out mine someday!

Laura Gill (9)
Portadown Integrated Primary School, Portadown

Not For Little Bird

Not for little bird the skies
Only air inside cage.
Not for little bird the worms,
Although he's filled with rage.

Not for little bird the space,
All warm on Market Street.
Not for little bird a branch
To rest his little feet.

Not for little bird the sun,
But darkness in his cage.
Not for little bird the freedom,
Except a show on stage.

Keelan Leeper (9)
Portadown Integrated Primary School, Portadown

Run Up To The Rugby World Cup

To get a ticket, they may be rare,
Even £2,000 a pair.
Go by plane, boat or bus,
Get there before the hassle and fuss.

Arrive in Paris for the match,
All the supporters ready to watch.
Hear the crowd, the way they cheer,
To give a better atmosphere.

All the players are fit and strong,
Habbanna and Monty won't get it wrong.
Drop-kicks, tries, penalties too,
They will get quite a few.

TV broken, planes are full,
The Internet is my best tool.
All the tickets, they have gone,
What a wait, it's far too long.

I've learnt the songs so I can rhyme,
Please hurry up, is it not time.
I'm so excited I cannot wait,
Which team will have the awful fate?

Allister McCord (9)
Portadown Integrated Primary School, Portadown

My Pumpkin

My pumpkin is orange, black and round,
And in my window he can be found
With a candle burning oh so bright,
He lights up the house on the darkest night.

Megan McLaughlin (8)
Portadown Integrated Primary School, Portadown

What Has Happened To Jack?

(Based on 'What Has Happened to Lulu?' by Charles Causley)

What has happened to Jack, Gibs?
What has happened to JA?
There's nothing in his bed except his captain's hat,
And a very *ugly picture of his ma!*

Why is his door unlocked, Gibs?
The rusty key still in its lock?
And only a shape on the dusty shelf where his pistol used to be,
He must be mad, he's not bad. Why did he take his clock?

Why do you turn your head, Gibs?
Why do grunts echo through the hall?
And why is the note never opened,
What does it say? I may never know at all.

Why do you wander about as though,
As though there's nothing wrong?
There is something wrong, I can tell.
Could Jack be gone?

Christopher Adams (10)
Portadown Integrated Primary School, Portadown

Cobra

Mine is the fang
That sends the venom,
That kills the heart.
Mine is the demon.

Mine are the wings
That people fear,
That they run away,
Mine is the jump of a spear.

Mine is the eye
That stares at his prey,
That is so scared.
Mine is the ray.

Sasha Thompson (9)
Portadown Integrated Primary School, Portadown

Two Shakes Of A Lamb's Tail

Two shakes of a lamb's tail
Is how long she takes
To post a letter to be mailed,
Then we get cake.

Two shakes of a lamb's tail
Is not so quick,
Sometimes it takes very long,
Not as quick as a wick.

Two shakes of a lamb's tail
At night,
Very dark,
She's out of my sight.

Two shakes of a lamb's tail,
Finally she is back in the car.
I told her I missed her.
She said she hadn't gone far.

Sarah Taylor (9)
Portadown Integrated Primary School, Portadown

Pop Star

Pop star, pop star, sing us a song,
Whilst we are all dancing along.
Disco lights shining bright
In the very dark disco night.

Backstage dancers dancing about
Whilst we all scream and shout.
Dance floors can't be seen
Because there are lots of dancing queens.

Costumes glittering in the light,
All the way to midnight.
Music playing really loud
Because there is a big crowd.

Rachel Kitchen (10)
Portadown Integrated Primary School, Portadown

Dingo Dog

Mine is the growl
That fulfils the bone,
In the cages at night,
Mine is the stone.

Mine is the eye
That sees in fear,
When cage men are here,
Mine is the clear.

Mine is the tail
That waddles around,
When cage men are by,
I stay unfound.

Abigail Tedford (10)
Portadown Integrated Primary School, Portadown

Der, The Duck

Quack, quack, quack,
I'm an intelligent duck,
I know lots of things,
Like clover means luck.

I'm very famous,
My intelligence is high,
Spend time doing research,
Never have I told a lie.

School is my favourite thing,
I even go to the after school.
I know all about God,
I think Satan is a fool.

Jack Richards (9)
Portadown Integrated Primary School, Portadown

What Has Happened To Bethany

(Based on 'What Has Happened to Lulu?' by Charles Causley)

What has happened to Bethany, Mother?
What has happened to Beth?
There's nothing in her room but a dressing gown on the door,
And some ugly clothes lying on the floor.

Why do you turn your head, Mother?
How come you don't go into her room anymore?
It doesn't seem the same,
You used to always do it before.

Why did Father start stripping the wallpaper?
It woke me up last night.
Why aren't you making nice dinners anymore?
I really feel like a bite.

Why are you always crying, Mother?
You say it's nothing at all
We always used to play together,
We really had a ball.

Bethany was the best,
I loved the juice she used to pour.
What has happened to Bethany, Mother?
What has happened to Beth?

Shannon Campbell (10)
Portadown Integrated Primary School, Portadown

Dog

Past his prime,
Wet nose,
Fluffy ears,
Dog sleeps.

Past his prime,
The dog is locked
In the cage,
His dripping tail.

Past his prime,
Locked up,
Lonely,
Sad.

Past his prime,
Dog is crying,
His ears dripping
With water
Where the rain comes in.

Past his prime
Dog lies,
Dog barks.

Jamie Lunt (10)
Portadown Integrated Primary School, Portadown

Spider!

Spiders live on the ground,
Spiders make you scurry around.
Little girls see spiders and scream,
Little boys think they're extreme.
Lots of spiders run really fast,
Lots of spiders never last,
Bang!

Deborah McCluskey (9)
St Bernadette's Primary School, Belfast

Caterpillar

C is for crawling
A is for amazing
T is for many types
E is for elegant
R is for robust
P is for precious
I is for interesting
L is for leaves
L is for long
A is for active
R is for resourceful.

Anna Keenan (8)
St Bernadette's Primary School, Belfast

Snails!

Snails are slimy,
As slimy as can be,
They slide around the garden,
One, two, three.

A snail looks like a slug
Carrying a stone,
But what a snail carries
Is a place called home.

Aimée Maguire (8)
St Bernadette's Primary School, Belfast

Bees

Bees are yellow and black,
Small and hairy,
Annoying and buzzing.
Honeybees are funny bees.
Bees drink the nectar out of flowers.

Nicole Muir (8)
St Bernadette's Primary School, Belfast

Mr Bee

Bumblebee, bumblebee
Flying around,
Looking for pollen
With a buzzing sound.

You find a big flower
With pollen for tea,
You suck it all up
To make sweet honey.

Annalise Warnock (9)
St Bernadette's Primary School, Belfast

Ladybirds

Look out for ladybirds,
They are a beautiful sight.
Light red, silver-yellow and
Light orange with black spots.
Ladybirds are the most
Helpful bug ever.
I love ladybirds.

Aisling Thompson (9)
St Bernadette's Primary School, Belfast

The Monster

This boy stinks,
He always blinks.
He is strong
But boy, what a pong!
A runny nose
And thick, long toes.
Don't make him mad
'Cause he'll be bad.
Beware of the monster!

Grace Guinness (7)
St Bride's Primary School, Belfast

The Ghost Lantern

I have a lantern and it is mine,
Nearly Hallowe'en time!
I use it here and there
To light up a nightmare.
On the night I lit it last,
A ghost came out from the past!
Everybody screamed and ran
And so did the frying pan!
After it was over,
Somebody had to eat clover.
Things may seem weird, but when you dream,
It's mean.

Rohan O'Hare (7)
St Bride's Primary School, Belfast

The Scary Ghost

On Hallowe'en night a tall boy was out for a walk.
As he walked, a scary ghost crept up behind him.
The ghost shouted, *'Boo!'*
The boy started to run away
And the ghost chased after him.
The ghost's breath was as smelly
As fried eggs and toast.
The boy said, 'I'm not afraid of you.'
Soon the moon started to come out
And it got very dark.

Niall Agnew (7)
St Bride's Primary School, Belfast

The Groton Of Kay

Smelly as a telly,
Spotty and dotty,
Running and humming
Faster and faster,
Making disaster.
Comes at midnight,
Sleeps in light.
His legs are black as emeralds -
Throw him out of sight,
He'll give you a fright.
They hunt with a dent in the head.
They should be dead!

Peter Heaney (7)
St Bride's Primary School, Belfast

My Elsandeer Monster

My elsandeer monster is really
A copy of an elf, Santa and a deer.
It always drinks beer.
It's met the writer of the book
'The Children of Lear'.
It likes to be near a tear,
It likes the road to be clear
'Cause it always gets knocked over.
Come and meet my elsandeer monster.

Callum Herity (8)
St Bride's Primary School, Belfast

Midnight

Did you know at midnight
Lots of children get a fright?
Spooky dreams on moonlit beams,
Lots of monsters and ghosts
With blood-dripping vampire hosts.
They keep saying they must eat Niall,
But will settle for a crocodile.
Watch out for a green spout,
Vampires are about!

Anna Sutherland (8)
St Bride's Primary School, Belfast

Wolfingstein

His teeth are as spiky as a pencil lead,
His hat is as black as a cat.
His ears smell like poo and
He has ten chubby arms.
His face is like a wolf.
His tail is as long as a rope.
His legs are as spiky as a nail.
His mouth is as small as an ant.

David Connolly (7)
St Bride's Primary School, Belfast

Untitled

He can burn your face.
He can fire up to space.
He is unbeatable.
He is weak when people
Put water on him.
He turns into ice.
Sometimes he can turn
Into a direct monster.

Tom Maguire (7)
St Bride's Primary School, Belfast

The Wicked Witch

The wicked witch,
As bold as a wolf,
With hair as thick as a book
And skin as green as grass!
Her cloak's as red as a cherry,
With clothes as black as a bat,
And fangs as sharp as razors,
But when you see her out in the sky,
You're sure to get a fright!

Damian Magee (8)
St Bride's Primary School, Belfast

The Weird Pumpkin

He had spiky hair as green as grass.
His hairy ears were dipped in blood!
Shiny silver spiky wings, sharp as a knife.
His body was a ghost.
His nails were sharp just like a harp.
His eyes were like metal.
His fingers were like spiders' legs.

Abhirami Santhosh Pillai (7)
St Bride's Primary School, Belfast

The Trouble With Smelly

His feet are big
And smellier than my feet.
He is big and small and dribbles.
Faster than me
Running as fast as I can.
He has big ears and can hear really well,
And has a little stinky nose.

Emer Megarity (7)
St Bride's Primary School, Belfast

The Cat Who Got Lost In The Snow

Once there was a cat
Who got lost in the snow.
His fur was brown,
Brown as the branch of a tree.
One night a witch came
And took the cat again.
Her eyes were blue,
Blue as the sky.
She was a girl
And her name was Ruby.

Ara McCartan (8)
St Bride's Primary School, Belfast

The Super Ghost

The ghost is a super man,
He drinks lots of Coke cans.
Sometimes he loves to dance,
He even likes to prance.
When he goes out for walks,
He always wants to talk.
When he goes home,
He always rings his phone.
That is what he is like,
So go and take a hike.

Paul Armstrong (8)
St Bride's Primary School, Belfast

Devil Princess

She's very, very mean,
Just like a queen.
She curls her hair
Just like a bear.
See her hair,
It's quite fair.
Her devil tail
Is like a nail.
She flies on her broomstick in the dark sky,
She's been and seen you watch her fly by.

Chloe Ireland (7)
St Bride's Primary School, Belfast

The Vampire

He is very smelly.
He wears a cloak.
His hair is spiky
And his teeth are bright red.
He snores when sleeping
But frightens you
When he wakes.
He eats slugs
And drinks blood.

Nikol Staikidou (8)
St Bride's Primary School, Belfast

Fairies

I know two fairies, they are cute.
They live in the trees, I go out to feed them.
By the way, it is a secret.
I know you won't tell.
They flutter about.
One has pink wings and the other has blue.
They are beautiful!

Did I tell you about the fairy queen and king?
They have a beautiful land.
I see them once a year.
The king is very handsome.
He is tall and proud.
The queen is the kindest person you have ever met.

Would you like to meet them?
If you wanted to see them, you have to believe in them.
Really believe in them, so you can see them.

Aoife Hollywood (7)
St Malachy's Primary School, Newry

My Irish Dancing

I love Irish dancing
More than anything I do.
I got a brand new costume
It's gold, red and blue.
I go to lessons twice a week
I practise when I'm there.
The favourite thing that I put on
Is my blonde wig for my hair
I wear it at the Feis.
For every dance I'm in
I point my toes and dance my best
And hope that I will win.

Roisin Cranney (8)
St Malachy's Primary School, Newry

On My First Day At School

On my first day at school
My dad left me.
I was feeling scared
I started to cry.
I wanted to know what it was like
When I walked into the classroom
It looked funny.

On my first day at school
My teacher was called Mrs Darragh
She showed us around the school.
My brother was in P5
 And my sister was in P7.

On my first day at school
It was break-time
And I played sharks with my friends
Then the bell went.

On my first day at school
We played in the water tank
As the day went past
I started to feel happier.

On my first day at school
It was nearly home time
We just played until home time
Then my mum and dad
Came and collected me.
They said, 'How was it?'
'Fine.'

Christopher McLaughlin (8)
St Mary's Primary School, Cushendall

The First Day At School

On my first day of school
My mummy took me into the classroom.
I saw the blackboard
I thought it was a deep hole
I saw the toilets, they were very small.

I heard the bell
And went to break.
I played with my friends
When the bell went
I did not know what to do
I panicked and shouted
'What do I do?'

Then I went inside
I copied everybody else
I played in the playhouse
And painted my house.
Then it was time to go home
My daddy picked me up
I was tired.

Conall McAteer (8)
St Mary's Primary School, Cushendall

My First Day At School

On my first day at school
I was very excited.
I saw all the books
There were lots of them.
I saw the teacher
She was very nice.

On my first day at school
I heard all the big children
They were very loud and noisy
I was a bit scared of them.
I played sharks in the playground
With my friends.

On my first day at school
I played with my friends
In the play shop.
I was very happy.
At the end of the day
I was very tired
And glad to get home.

Molly McLaughlin (8)
St Mary's Primary School, Cushendall

On My First Day At School

I saw the children and thought . . .
They're giants in uniform
What's that smell, is it soup?
No, it's called hot dog
Hot dog!
We have to eat a dog for lunch . . .

On my first day at school
I saw books, all types of books.
What is a book?
Is a book something you wear?
What is a blackboard?
It's a big black hole that sucks us in!

On my first day at school
We did some colouring and painting.
I put some paint on my paper
I made a painting of a flower.

On my first day at school
Soon it was time to go home
I didn't want to go
Mum said I had to go
We had to walk all the way to the car.
I was so tired I almost fell asleep
In the car to my nana's house.

Holly Fleet (9)
St Mary's Primary School, Cushendall

My First Day At School

On my first day at school
I was very scared.
My mum told me
And my brother was too.
I sort of recovered my ability
To confront my fear.
My mum thought I was being a bit silly.

On my first day at school
When I got to the playground
I wondered if the teacher
Was scary or good.
Or was it the classmates
Who were mean and rude?

On my first day at school
I heard the bell go
We went outside.
I brought my whole lunch out
Everyone else didn't.

On my first day at school
The bell rang one more time
Then we went home.
Mum said, 'How was school?'
I said it was brilliant.

Ciaran Quinn (9)
St Mary's Primary School, Cushendall

My First Day At School

On my first day at school
I went into the classroom
And said hello, in a squeaky voice.
Adam, Dealan
And Laoiseachrua
Looked round at
Me and
Said hi.

We played dress-
Ups together and
Had great, great,
Great fun
Together.

At the end of the
Day I was *very*
Tired.
I heard the
Other kids say
Hello to their
Mums and dads.
I saw my mum
I cried out 'Mum'
I ran to
Her
She took me home.

Declan Thompson (9)
St Mary's Primary School, Cushendall

My First Day At School

On my first day at school,
I was very, very shy
Because I thought I wouldn't know anyone,
The teacher said, 'Hello Cliodhna,'
I was confused, I thought she would take me away.

On my first day at school,
The teacher told us her name,
She was called Mrs Darragh.
We got a tour around the school
I saw my brother and sister
And they said hello.

On my first day at school,
Soon it was break time
I played with Siobhan and Molly
I knew Siobhan before nursery,
We played on the big hill together
We had lots of fun playing.

On my first day at school,
After break Miss Darragh let us paint
I painted a picture
Of me and my friends,
I got along with the other children
And soon we were friends.
It was soon home time
And I had a great time.

Cliodhna McManus (8)
St Mary's Primary School, Cushendall

My First Day At School

On my first day at school
I walked through the door
And all these people stared.
I was very nervous and worried
But my granny was a friend with the teacher,
She was called Mrs Darragh
And I liked her because she was nice.
I sat beside my friend Cliodhna
And Molly was at the table too.

On my first day at school
My friends and I talked to each other
We were having fun.
Tegan showed me a TV
I was wondering why there was a TV
Did you watch TV in school?
I was sad my friend Kirsty wasn't there.

On my first day at school
There were tables that were funny shapes.
At break I was scared to go out
But when I went outside
I played a game.
At first I couldn't understand it
But then I got the hang of it.
It was called Sharks and was really good.
At home time we said our prayer.
I wanted to go there tomorrow again
It was great fun.

Siobhan McKillop (8)
St Mary's Primary School, Cushendall

Hallowe'en Is Coming

Hallowe'en is coming
Witches and ghosts
Come to play.

Fireworks and bonfires
Big lights in the air
Hallowe'en is here now.

Children trick or treating
Sweets and monkey nuts
All nice in my tummy.

I love Hallowe'en
It is a great time
For children and adults.

But then Hallowe'en is over
We go to bed
That is Hallowe'en.

Orlaith McAlister (10)
St Mary's Primary School, Cushendall

Autumn Leaves

Leaves are falling on the ground
They flutter and they blow around
They spin and twirl without a sound
Forming carpets on the ground.

Some are red and some are brown
Autumn leaves are tumbling down.

Paul Emerson (10)
St Mary's Primary School, Cushendall

My First Day At School

On my first day at school
I saw children that I never met before.
A dog came into our classroom
I was dying to pet it
But the teacher took it away.
I saw play cars and asked
Could I play with them
The teacher said yes.

On my first day at school
At playtime me and my friends
Played red rover and chases.
At that time a bell went
I didn't know what to do.
The P2s lined up
I didn't know to do the same
I just played on.
The teacher came out and told us to line up.

On my first day at school
Mrs Darragh read a story about bears.
When she finished
It was time to go home.
My mum came to collect me.
She said, 'Did you have a good time?'
'Yes, I had a great time.'

Liam Gillan (8)
St Mary's Primary School, Cushendall

My First Day At School

On my first day at school
Walking through the playground,
I saw a boy and asked him what primary one was like.
He told me there were monsters, books that eat you up,
Flying carpets and a teacher who looks like a pink marshmallow.
I started to get scared
So I went into the classroom
But the teacher wasn't a marshmallow
She was a lovely red rose.
I still think there are monsters
And the teacher's name was Miss Honey.

On my first day at school
I was playing with my friends in the sand,
The teacher was nice
But I was still unsure.
I wondered what my mum was doing
Doing something fun,
Like playing on the trampoline.

On my first day at school
Getting ready to go home
The bell rang and it was time to go.
Mum came and picked me up
I felt tired so I fell asleep in the car.

Tegan Walker (9)
St Mary's Primary School, Cushendall

My First Day At School

On my first day at school
I was very scared.
I always heard toilets flushing.
I thought I was going to
Get eaten up by the table.
I scribbled on my first bit of work.
We started to paint.
I painted me as Superman.

On my first day at school
I smelt the crayons.
They smelt weird.
The toilets smelt like sewers.
My brothers said monsters came out
Of the toilets to clean them.
I felt scared after my brother said it.

On my first day at school
I liked the teacher.
She was kind and friendly.
I never wanted to leave her class.
At lunchtime
Me and my friends played chasing.

On my first day at school
I walked home.
I was tired and fell onto my sofa
Fast asleep.

Oran McCarthy (9)
St Mary's Primary School, Cushendall

My First Day At School

On my first day at school,
My mummy and daddy
Brought me into the classroom.
I saw the cloakroom, it scared me.
When the bell rang for break
It made me jump!

On my first day at school,
I walked into the playground.
When I saw the shelters
They looked scary.
A big boy said, 'Are you going into primary one?'
I said yes
Quietly.

On my first day at school,
The P5's looked big
And started to scare me.
It started to make me nervous.
I got into class and Mummy went away.
I sneaked out of the classroom
And went to the window
And said, 'Come and catch me!'

On my first day at school,
We went for PE and we played
With the PE toys.
At last it was time to go home.
Daddy came and picked me up.
I was tired.

Jane Emerson (9)
St Mary's Primary School, Cushendall

Hallowe'en Ball

Skulls and skeletons
Get off the houses' walls
And they go to get ready
For the Hallowe'en ball.

Witches and warlocks are
Getting ready to dance
While the pumpkin and the
Cat do the cha-cha dance.

The Hallowe'en ball is over now
Creatures scare kids
Out of their homes.

Children run and scream
And they mess about.

That is what I call
The best Hallowe'en ever.

Roisin Healy (10)
St Mary's Primary School, Cushendall

I Went For A Walk

I went for a walk one day
It was about the end of May.
I walked all the way to Waterfoot Bay.
I went to the chapel to pray for Papa K
To make the pain in his leg go away.
I walked back the same way.
I heard a boy Ray say,
'Does anyone pay for a bale of hay?'
I saw a hen lay an egg
And say cluck cluck today.
I walked away.
I knew I was home when I heard Papa say
'Tay, tay. Hurry up, do not delay.'

Fiona McDonnell (9)
St Mary's Primary School, Cushendall

My First Day At School

On my first day at school
I saw big boys and girls
They were running across the yard.
I was walking to school
It was a windy day.

On my first day at school
I though it was going to rain.
The teacher said,
'Hello, it is good to see you.'
My mummy walked away
I was about to cry.

On my first day at school
My teacher said,
'Don't cry, school is over at 2 o'clock.'
Finally 2 o'clock came
I was tired and wanted to go home.
'Did you like school today?' Mum asked.
'No,' I said.
I ran to my mum.
Mum said, 'Why are you running?'
I said, 'The teacher scared me.
Do I have to go to school tomorrow?'

Daniel O'Boyle (8)
St Mary's Primary School, Cushendall

My First Day At School

On my first day at school
I was in the car with Mum and Dad.
Mummy said, 'I hope you enjoy school.'
Mummy said, 'Mrs Darragh is a good friend.'

On my first day at school
I walked into the playground.
Big boys and girls were running very fast.
I was excited and scared.
Mummy said, 'Goodbye.'
I didn't want Mummy to go home.
We played games like red rover in the playground.
The bell went off, I saw the P2s lined up,
I didn't know to line up
So I just played on.

On my first day at school
I asked Mrs Darragh,
'What time do we go home?'
She said, '2 o'clock.'
When it was time to go home
We all said goodbye to Mrs Darragh
And walked out of the classroom.
I saw Mummy and ran to her.
She asked me, 'How was school?'
I said, *'Very good!'*

Orla Delargy (9)
St Mary's Primary School, Cushendall

My First Day At School

On my first day at school
I was scared
Because I thought the teacher
Would be scary.

On my first day at school
I saw Mrs Darragh
And she said, 'Hello Scott.'
I was nervous.

On my first day at school
I played games with my friends
We played hide-and-seek
In the playground.
Ciaran was it.

On my first day at school
Dinner was nice
Then went home at 2.00
My dad said, 'How was school?'
I said, 'It was good.'

Scott Walsh (8)
St Mary's Primary School, Cushendall

My First Day At School

On my first day at school
I was a bit scared.
I thought I would do something wrong
And I didn't want to go in.

The chalk looked like smoke.
Mrs Darragh let us play with some toys.
I was very happy now.

Soon it was lunchtime.
I got my lunch box.
We got to eat our lunch in the classroom.
After lunch Mrs Darragh read us a story.
I was glad I went to school.

Then it was home time.
Dad took me home and I had tea.
I was sad to leave school.

Lauren Ghio (8)
St Mary's Primary School, Cushendall

Happiness

Happiness smells like a river of joy.
Happiness sounds like a choir of angels.
Happiness feels like Christmas Day.
Happiness tastes like a box of strawberries.
Happiness looks like a picture of love.
Happiness reminds me of playing with all my friends.
I like happiness because if you don't have happiness you'll be angry.
I wish happiness were a big, big box of chocolates.

Danaé Marron (10)
St Oliver Plunkett's Primary School, Toomebridge

Seasons In A Box

When I opened my autumn box out streamed . . .
Orange crumpled leaves,
Animals hibernating,
Sparkling acorns,
Shorter days,
Longer nights.

When I opened my winter box out streamed . . .
Lots of snowmen,
People getting Christmas presents,
Children playing in the snow,
Water freezing into ice,
Everyone having snowball fights.

When I opened my spring box out streamed . . .
Lots of flowers,
New baby lambs born,
People cutting lawns,
Clocks going forward.

When I opened my summer box out streamed . . .
Splashing water fights,
Lots of new movies,
Going to the pool,
People going on holiday.

Jamie Donaghy (9)
St Oliver Plunkett's Primary School, Toomebridge

Forgiveness

The colour of forgiveness is pink like a cuddly pink teddy bear.
I wish forgiveness was that everyone loved each other eternally.
Forgiveness smells like a pink rose.
Forgiveness sounds like when the teacher says,
'You're the best in the class.'
Forgiveness looks like people hugging.
Forgiveness reminds me of everyone together like a happy family.

Niamh Bovill (9)
St Oliver Plunkett's Primary School, Toomebridge

Seasons In A Box

When I opened my autumn box out streamed:
Crispy leaves,
Acorns dropping,
Cracking conkers,
Foxes hunting for food.

When I opened my winter box out streamed:
A cold snowman standing alone,
Slippery roads,
Kids playing with snow,
Warm clothes,
Frosty windows with patterns.

When I opened my spring box out streamed:
Lambs being born,
Easter coming,
Flowers growing,
Spring cleaning,
Snowdrops bursting open.

When I opened my summer box out streamed:
Sunshine smiling on everyone,
Water fights with friends,
Swimming pool trips,
Ice cream to cool us down,
Water slides in the garden.

Elena Hill (10)
St Oliver Plunkett's Primary School, Toomebridge

Seasons In A Box

When I opened my autumn box out streamed . . .
Dry crispy leaves,
Days that are shorter,
Acorns thumping on the ground,
Wetter days,
Badgers hibernating.

When I opened my winter box out streamed . . .
Santa Claus,
Snowball fights,
A white blanket of snow,
Trees with no leaves, bare and cold,
Snowmen up tall.

When I opened my spring box out streamed . . .
Skipping lambs,
Lovely sunny days,
Birds building nests,
Buds bursting open,
Animals waking from their winter sleep,
Days back to normal after winter.

When I opened my summer box out streamed . . .
Lovely green leaves and summer flowers,
Days that are longer and warmer sunshine,
Children playing outside,
Hooray summer holidays!

Bryan Letters (9)
St Oliver Plunkett's Primary School, Toomebridge

Seasons In A Box

When I opened my winter box out streamed:
Cold weather, short days,
Snow falling,
Bare trees and hedges,
Very few birds,
Christmas time and giving presents.

When I opened my spring box out streamed:
Lambs jumping
Longer days, warmer weather,
Easter time with Easter eggs,
Daffodils blooming,
Birds building nests and laying eggs.

When I opened my summer box out streamed:
Hot weather,
People eating ice creams,
Lazy days on the beach,
Farmers making hay,
Long, bright days.

When I opened my autumn box out streamed:
Golden leaves,
Nuts ripening on the trees,
Squirrels hibernating,
Bonfires, fireworks and trick or treating.

Clodagh Scullion (9)
St Oliver Plunkett's Primary School, Toomebridge

Seasons In A Box

When I opened my autumn box out streamed:
Crumpled leaves,
Brown cracking conkers,
The colours scarlet, crimson, golden, amber and russet of leaves,
Animals hibernating.

When I opened my winter box out streamed:
Freezing cold weather,
Snow falling from the sky,
Loads of presents,
Christmas trees,
Santa coming,
Jesus' birthday.

When I opened my spring box out streamed:
Flowers starting to bloom,
Birds singing,
A small white ball with four legs,
A fluffy tail hopping in the field,
Longer days.

When I opened my summer box out streamed:
Lovely bright sunlight,
Gaelic started again,
Going to the beach,
Going on holiday,
Lovely ice cream,
Out of school for two months.

Paul Tohill (10)
St Oliver Plunkett's Primary School, Toomebridge

Seasons In A Box

When I opened my autumn box out streamed . . .
Crumpled colourful leaves,
Trees shedding leaves,
Acorns dropping,
Crackling conkers,
Squirrels collecting nuts,
Cooler weather.

When I opened my winter box out streamed . . .
Snowball fights,
Snow falling in a blizzard,
Hailstones rattling and bouncing on the ground,
Santa coming with presents,
Dinner being eaten,
Animals hibernating,
Jingling bells ringing.

When I opened my spring box out streamed . . .
Flowers blooming,
Buds growing,
People playing,
Grass growing,
Lambs being born,
People running and having fun.

When I opened my summer box out streamed . . .
A big orange sun,
People playing and having fun,
Water fights and people going on holiday,
Splashing pools of nice cool water to play with.

James McFall (10)
St Oliver Plunkett's Primary School, Toomebridge

Love

Love is scarlet-red.
I wish love was a medicine you take when you are angry,
Love looks like your mum and dad talking and laughing,
Love tastes like hot chocolate,
Love sounds like birds chirping a happy song,
Love reminds me of sad movies like the 'Crucifixion',
Love feels like a soft fluffy teddy,
I like love because it is like cupid hitting you with an arrow.

Shannon McCann (10)
St Oliver Plunkett's Primary School, Toomebridge

Hate

Hate smells like manure,
Hate sounds like scraping a plate with a fork,
Hate feels like scratching the blackboard,
Hate reminds me of breaking my arm,
Hate tastes like red tomatoes,
I wish hate would end,
Hate looks like a bully,
I dislike it because it annoys people.

Luke McCoy (9)
St Oliver Plunkett's Primary School, Toomebridge

Happiness

Happiness is bright yellow
It sounds like a bluebird singing sweetly
It tastes like melting ice cream
It smells like a big, blooming flower
It looks like the sun shining brightly
It feels like a soft blanket
It reminds me of a warm, glowing fire.

Dione Kelly (10)
St Patrick's Primary School, Aughacommon

Fear!

Fear is yellow with a hint of red,
It sounds like a child screaming in bed,
It tastes like sour milk flowing through your head,
It smells like a cigarette freshly made,
It looks like a tarantula's big freaky head,
It feels like a very harsh death,
It reminds me of an ogre's stinky breath!

Fearghal Hosty-Blaney (10)
St Patrick's Primary School, Aughacommon

Happiness

Happiness is bright pink.
It sounds like a bird singing sweetly.
It tastes like hot, melting chocolate.
It smells like a colourful flower.
It looks like a laughing child playing.
It feels like a soft teddy.
It reminds me of children having fun.

Megan Doyle (10)
St Patrick's Primary School, Aughacommon

Love

Love is bright orange
It sounds like sizzling bacon
It tastes like fried sausages
It smells like fresh air
It looks like a perfect picture
it feels like a soft chair
It reminds me of holidays.

Matthew McCabe (10)
St Patrick's Primary School, Aughacommon

Happiness

Happiness is rosy pink.
It sounds like children laughing in the park.
It tastes like creamy chocolate.
It smells like fresh flowers.
It looks like the waves gently flowing over the sand.
It feels like a woolly sheep.
It reminds me of a Saturday morning when I get up
And then realise I have no school.

Meadhbh O'Neill (10)
St Patrick's Primary School, Aughacommon

Happiness

Happiness is yellow.
It sounds like children crying.
It tastes like ice cream on a sunny day.
It smells like sunflowers in a garden.
It looks like a person smiling.
It feels like a leather chair in a car.
It reminds me of sleeping in on a Saturday morning.

Caolan Farrell (10)
St Patrick's Primary School, Aughacommon

Love

Love is rosy red
It sounds like birds singing in a tree
It tastes like melted chocolate
It smells like delicious Sunday dinner
It looks like a red rose in bloom
It feels like a fluffy pillow
It reminds me of my family.

Eimear Neeson (10)
St Patrick's Primary School, Aughacommon

Fear

Fear is red like fire.
It smells like broccoli.
It tastes like turnip.
Fear looks like a knife.
It feels rough like rocks.
Fear lives in my body when I am scared.
It sounds like tyres screeching on a car.
It reminds me of a forest.

Liam Coleman (9)
St Patrick's Primary School, Aughacommon

Happiness

Happiness is bright blue.
It sounds like cows mooing.
It tastes like warm melting chocolate.
It smells like celebrity perfume.
It looks like a bright sun.
It feels like a soft towel.
It reminds me of people smiling.

Aoibhin McCarron (10)
St Patrick's Primary School, Aughacommon

Happiness

Happiness is the colour blue
It sounds like marvellous music
It tastes like mouth-watering chocolate
It smells like air freshener
It looks like green smoke
It feels like a smooth blanket
It reminds me of a film.

Callum Doran (10)
St Patrick's Primary School, Aughacommon

Fear

Fear is light blue like the sky.
It tastes like a bloody cut.
Fear is when your eyes are wide open.
Fear is ruby red.
It reminds me about things that bump during the night.
It looks like iron gates on an old house.
It sounds like thunder on a bad day.
Fear lives in your brain.

Kerry McGibbon (9)
St Patrick's Primary School, Aughacommon

Happiness

Happiness is yellow like the sun,
It smells like perfume,
It looks like a circle of bananas,
Happiness is autumn leaves dancing,
It sounds like sweet music,
It tastes like strawberries,
It feels like soft pyjamas.

Wiktoria Wylecial (9)
St Patrick's Primary School, Aughacommon

Hate

Hate is red like blood,
It tastes like turnip,
Hate smells like dust blowing in the air,
It sounds like thunder on a dark, cold night,
Hate feels like somebody is falling on a stony hard ground,
Hate lives in bullying.

Jane Douglas (9)
St Patrick's Primary School, Aughacommon

Anger

Anger is dark blue like under the sea
And is as dark as a blue sky.
It feels as if you were drowning.
Anger tastes likes salt water.
It smells like fried bacon.
It looks as brown as a burnt sausage.
It sounds like a rumbling noise.
It lives in my body.

Tiarnan Kane (9)
St Patrick's Primary School, Aughacommon

Anger

Anger is red like red-hot lava in a volcano
It smells like rotten eggs
Anger tastes like horrible bitterness
It sounds like a loud screech
Anger feels like thorns withering away
It lives deep in your heart
Anger reminds me of sourness.

Owen McConville (9)
St Patrick's Primary School, Aughacommon

Silence

Silence is white like the clouds.
It tastes like a piece of cheese.
Silence looks like a quiet person.
It lives in the chapel.
Silence reminds me of the open air.
Silence smells fresh and sweet.
Silence sounds like a library.

Tiarnan Geddis (9)
St Patrick's Primary School, Aughacommon

Fear

Fear is black like a cold night sky,
It feels like your body is clogging up with disease and hatred,
It tastes like sour and bitter oranges,
Fear sounds like a howl of a wolf at the moon,
It looks like a boat sinking, car crashing,
Fear reminds me of a forest and me all alone in it,
Fear lives deep in your heart,
Fear smells like a smoky fire.

Jamie Hogan (9)
St Patrick's Primary School, Aughacommon

Hunger

Hunger is green like grass.
It smells like a Sunday dinner.
Hunger tastes like a bag of salt and vinegar crisps.
It sounds like your tummy rumbling like a drum.
It feels like emptiness in your stomach.
Hunger lives in your stomach.
It reminds me of the days in school.
Hunger looks like a round ball.

James McAlinden (9)
St Patrick's Primary School, Aughacommon

Love

Love is red like love hearts,
It tastes like sugary sweets,
It smells like new-bloomed roses,
Love sounds like gentleness on a beach,
It feels excited and bubbly in your stomach,
Love lives in your heart, top to bottom,
It's a very strong feeling,
Love reminds me of being adored and cared for.

Chloe Austin (9)
St Patrick's Primary School, Aughacommon

Fun

Fun is soft, pink candyfloss.
It smells like crimson red roses with a perfume tinge.
Fun tastes like strawberries and cream on the top of your tongue.
It sounds like children playing in the street.
Fun feels like happiness, laughter and joy.
Fun lives in your heart, a beautiful emotion.
It looks like a fluffy dog.
Fun reminds me of the times I love life!

Laura McStay (9)
St Patrick's Primary School, Aughacommon

Sadness

Sadness is dark green cabbage,
It feels like thorns pouring down on me,
Sadness smells like bad air coming through you,
It sounds like people crying,
Sadness tastes like raw ice cream melting,
Sadness feels like someone dying in your arms,
It lives in the air far, far away,
It looks like a whole place of sadness,
It reminds me of a friend helping me.

Eamon Coleman (9)
St Patrick's Primary School, Aughacommon

Happiness

Happiness is cheerful like me,
It's pink like Barney the dinosaur,
It smells like my mum's perfume,
It tastes of fresh scrambled eggs in the microwave,
It sounds like everybody loves you,
It feels like hearts growing inside your body,
It reminds you of snuggling up in your pyjamas.

Alex McConville (9)
St Patrick's Primary School, Aughacommon

Laughter

Laughter is yellow like a sunflower,
It reminds me of the hot sun shining down on me,
It looks like a girl jumping up and down on her trampoline,
It smells like perfume,
It tastes like hard sweets,
It feels like a warm breeze,
It sounds like people making you laugh!

Hannah McDowell (9)
St Patrick's Primary School, Aughacommon

Laughter

Laughter is violet with a little light glow,
It sounds like children playing in the snow,
It tastes like chocolate filled with cream,
It smells like painted skateboards going to extreme,
It looks like a child smiling inside,
It feels like water coming in with the tide,
It reminds me of something great, but small,
Laughter is fun and joy for all.

Bláthnaid McCaughley (10)
St Patrick's Primary School, Aughacommon

Fun

Fun is red like a fresh rose,
Fun smells like perfume,
It tastes like sweets and chocolate,
It sounds like laughter and happiness,
It feels like joy in your body,
It lives around you and in you,
Fun reminds you of playing outside with your friends.

Emer Haughian (9)
St Patrick's Primary School, Aughacommon

Fear

Fear is black, bold and dark.
It sounds like screaming in the night.
It tastes like burnt crisps, horrible and sickening.
It smells like smoke, contaminating all life.
It looks like a monster, misunderstood but scary.
It feels like dry glue, hard and old.
It reminds me of nightmares and horrors, scary and horrible.

Conor McKerr (9)
St Patrick's Primary School, Aughacommon

Happiness

Happiness is green
It sounds like screams in Old Trafford
It tastes like a spicy chicken pizza
It smells like a footballer's changing room after a match
It looks like a magnificent display of fireworks
It feels like a leather chair in the house
It reminds me of watching TV on a Friday night.

Brandon O'Neill (10)
St Patrick's Primary School, Aughacommon

Love

Love is red like red lipstick.
Red boiling soup smells like hot and lovely.
Soup would taste lovely and fantastic.
It sounds like the pot would blow in the pot.
It would be really chilly and hot.

Christopher Breen (9)
St Patrick's Primary School, Aughacommon

Happiness

Happiness is blue
It sounds like birds singing in the morning
It tastes like chips
It smells like fresh air blowing in my face
It looks like people having fun
It feels like me touching a leather chair in a limo
It reminds me of going to Manchester for my holiday.

Conor Conway (10)
St Patrick's Primary School, Aughacommon

Happiness

Happiness is bright yellow,
It sounds like relaxing music,
It tastes like fresh cookies,
It smells like sweet perfume,
It looks like a glowing sunset in June,
It feels like fluffy fur,
It reminds me of being with my friends.

Carla Gormley (10)
St Patrick's Primary School, Aughacommon

The Shiny Moon

A blacky yellow bee whizzing through the air
Shiny bright stars dancing
The moon shining to the Earth
Butterflies flying through the wind
Then the sun rises
The moon and stars disappear.

Oisin Maginness (10)
Saints & Scholars Integrated Primary & Nursery School, Armagh

My Ladybird

My beautiful ladybird
No smaller than my hand
As beautiful as a flower
It's the most beautiful thing I have ever seen
It comes to me each morning
It looks at me and smiles and that is my ladybird
The loveliest thing I have ever seen.

Maeve McSorley (9)
Saints & Scholars Integrated Primary & Nursery School, Armagh

Hallowe'en

Trouble, trouble, cauldron bubble
Spider's head very hairy
Skin of rat, very furry
Dogs' big eyes and frogs' thick legs
Worms' body smells all day
Lizard's foot rots away
Popping, banging, glooping, hissing
Trouble, trouble, cauldron bubble.

Michael Scott (10)
Strand Primary School, Belfast

Hallowe'en

Boil, boil, trouble double
Fire hiss and cauldron bubble.
Iguana's leg and wasp's sting
Rat's blood and bat's wing.
Poisoned entrails and slow worm's tail
Snake's eye and monkey's nail,
Boil, boil, trouble double
Fire hiss and cauldron bubble.

Shane Rutherford (9)
Strand Primary School, Belfast

Hallowe'en

Bubble, bubble, cook up trouble
In the cauldron bubble, bubble
In goes slimy salamander tails
And twenty-eight crocodile scales
After that go teachers' heads
And some sticky spiderwebs
Then add a croak of seven frogs
And a drop of blood from dogs
The tail of a skunk
A sting of a wasp
Bubble, bubble, cook up trouble
In the cauldron bubble, bubble.

Ben Clark (9)
Strand Primary School, Belfast

Hallowe'en

Bubble, bubble, double trouble
Fire burn and cauldron sizzle
A tail of a rat
A top of a hat
A head of a mouse
Which lives in a house
A leg of a dog
A toe of a frog
A donkey's ear
And a tail of deer
Bubble, bubble, double trouble
Fire burn and cauldron sizzle.

Claire Laverty (10)
Strand Primary School, Belfast

Hallowe'en

Bubbling, bubbling, popping and banging
Fire grizzling and cauldron sizzling
Wet dog's snotty nose
Hairy spiders' legs and toes
Hissing, steaming around the pot
Sloppy, dirty owls' feet
Gathered from the stinky street
Booming, popping, hissing sound
Stir and stir it all around
Bubbling, bubbling, popping and banging
Fire grizzling and cauldron sizzling.

Aimee Chapman
Strand Primary School, Belfast

Hallowe'en

Hubble, hubble this and that
Poppedy, poppedy, hiss and zap!
Elephant's trunk, eight rat eyes
In they go and here's a surprise!
10 donkey nails all mixed with snails
4 crocodiles' teeth and 3 cows' tails
Hubble, hubble this and that
Poppedy, poppedy, hiss and zap!

Hannah Killen
Strand Primary School, Belfast

Hallowe'en

Bubble, bubble, beware of trouble,
Cauldron was springing while the witch was singing,
A head of a dog,
The tongue of a frog,
The horn of a deer,
With a donkey's ear.
The beak of a duck,
With some garden muck.
The hair of a bear
And some rabbit fur.
Bubble, bubble, beware of trouble,
Cauldron was springing while the witch was singing!

Ross Carvill (9)
Strand Primary School, Belfast

Hallowe'en

Double, double, pop and trouble
Fire sizzling and cauldron bubble
A slimy slug and some dirt
A rat's long tail and a dog's little toe
A hamster's nose and eye of a cat
Stir it all up
And that is that
Double, double, pop and trouble
Fire sizzling and cauldron bubble.

Natalie McMaster (10)
Strand Primary School, Belfast

Young Writers Information

We hope you have enjoyed reading this book - and that you will continue to enjoy it in the coming years.

If you like reading and writing poetry drop us a line, or give us a call, and we'll send you a free information pack.

Alternatively if you would like to order further copies of this book or any of our other titles, then please give us a call or log onto our website at www.youngwriters.co.uk

Young Writers Information
Remus House
Coltsfoot Drive
Peterborough
PE2 9JX

(01733) 890066